ENJOY YOUR JOURNEY

ENJOY YOUR JOURNEY

Find the Treasure Hidden in Every Day

JOYCE MEYER

HODDER &
STOUGHTON

Unless otherwise indicated, all Scripture quotations are taken from *The Amplified Bible, Classic Edition* (AMPC). *Old Testament* copyright © 1965, 1987 by The Zondervan Corporation, Grand Rapids, Michigan. *New Testament* copyright © 1958, 1987 by The Lockman Foundation. Used by permission.

Some Scripture quotations marked Ben Campbell Johnson Paraphrase are taken from *Luke and John, An Interpretive Paraphrase* by Ben Campbell Johnson, © 1980, A Great Love, Inc.; *Matthew and Mark, A Relational Paraphrase* by Ben Campbell Johnson, © 1978, A Great Love, Inc.; or *The Heart of Paul, Biblical Truth in Today's Language* by Ben Campbell Johnson, © 1976, A GreatLove, Inc.

Scripture quotations marked KJV are taken from the King James Version of the Bible. Scripture quotations marked NKJV are taken from The New King James Version of the Bible. Copyright © 1979,1980,1982 by Thomas Nelson, Inc., Publishers.

Published in association with FaithWords, a division of Hachette Book Group USA, Inc.

Originally published in 1996 under the title *Enjoying Where You Are*
This abridged edition first published in July 2017

First published in Great Britain in 2017 by Hodder & Stoughton
An Hachette UK company

2

Copyright © Joyce Meyer, 1996, 2017

A CIP catalogue record for this title is available from the British Library

ISBN 978 1 473 66335 0
eBook ISBN 978 1 473 66336 7

Printed and bound in the UK by Clays Ltd, Elcograf S.p.A.

Hodder & Stoughton policy is to use papers that are natural, renewable and recyclable products and made from wood grown in sustainable forests. The logging and manufacturing processes are expected to conform to the environmental regulations of the country of origin.

Hodder & Stoughton Ltd
Carmelite House
50 Victoria Embankment
London EC4Y 0DZ

www.hodderfaith.com

CONTENTS

CONTENTS

INTRODUCTION

I believe that life should be a celebration. Far too many people don't even enjoy life, let alone celebrate it. I frequently say that many people are on their way to heaven, but very few are enjoying the trip. For many years I was one of those people.

But thankfully, God has taught me a great deal about how to enjoy life. Through His grace, God has shown me that the life He has given us is meant to be enjoyed. Jesus came that we might **have and enjoy life, and have it in abundance (to the full, till it overflows)** according to *The Amplified Bible, Classic Edition* version of John 10:10. There are many other similar Scriptures in the Bible that I will expound on in this book that show us it is God's will for us to enjoy every day of our lives.

I believe that reading this book may be life-changing for you. Perhaps you are as I was at one time. You truly love the Lord with all your heart and are trying so hard to please Him that you are forgetting to live the full the abundant life He has provided.

Enjoyment of life is not based on enjoyable circumstances;

it's an attitude of the heart, a decision to enjoy everything because everything—even little, seemingly insignificant things—have a part in the overall "big picture" of life.

When I finally realized that I was not enjoying my life, I had to make a quality decision to find out what was wrong and rectify it. This decision demanded learning new ways of handling situations.

Once I discovered that the world was not going to change, I decided that it was my approach to some of the "lemons" in life that needed adjustment. I had heard someone say that lemons can make us sour or we can turn them into lemonade. My decision to make lemonade instead of turning sour required that I learn balance in my work habits.

I was a workaholic who found great satisfaction in accomplishment. Of course, God desires and even commands us to bear fruit. We should not waste time and be "do-nothings," but an unbalanced attitude in this area causes many people to experience burnout from a lifestyle of all work and no play. I was one of those people. Actually, I didn't know how to play and truly enjoy it. I always felt I should be working. I felt safe only when I was doing something "constructive."

I also had to change my attitude toward people. I learned that one of the reasons I didn't enjoy life was because I didn't enjoy most of the people in my life. I was trying to change them so I would find them enjoyable instead of accepting them the way they were and enjoying them while God was changing them.

I believe that all of us truly need teaching on this subject of how to enjoy where we are on the way to where we are going. I pray that this book will be a major blessing in your life, and that, as you read it, God will bring you to a crossroads—a place of decision—where you can choose to begin celebrating life—every day.

1

Life Is a Journey

The thief comes only in order to steal and kill and destroy. I came that they may have and enjoy life, and have it in abundance (to the full, till it overflows).

John 10:10

I have come to realize that there is nothing as tragic as being alive and not enjoying life. I wasted much of my own life because I did not know how to enjoy where I was while I was on the way to where I was going.

Life is a journey. Everything in it is a process. It has a beginning, a middle and an end. All aspects of life are always developing. Life is motion. Without movement, advancement and progression, there is no life. Once a thing has ceased to progress, it is dead.

In other words, as long as you and I are alive, we are always going to be going somewhere. We are created by God to be goal-oriented visionaries. Without a vision, we atrophy and become bored and hopeless. We need to have something to reach for, but in the reaching toward what lies ahead in the *future,* we must not lose sight of the *now!*

I think this principle applies to every area of life, but let's look at just one of those areas. Let's say an unsaved person who has no relationship with God becomes aware that something is missing in his life and so he starts searching. The Holy Spirit draws him to the place where he is confronted with making a decision about placing his faith in Christ. So he accepts God and then moves from the place of searching for an unknown something to discovering who that something is. In so doing, he enters a temporary place of satisfaction and fulfillment.

Please notice that I said *temporary,* because soon the Holy Spirit will begin drawing him to press on to a deeper place in God. The process of conviction of sin will begin in his daily life through the presence of the Holy Spirit, who is the Revealer of truth (John 14:16-17), working continually in and with the believer to bring him into new levels of awareness. And entering a new level always means leaving an old one behind.

We are always heading somewhere spiritually, and we should be enjoying the journey. We should enjoy the place where we are—even as we keep moving forward in our relationship with God. Seeking God's will for our lives—allowing Him to deal with us about attitudes and issues, desiring to know His plan for our lives and fulfilling it—all these things are part of the journey of Christianity.

"Desiring" and "seeking" are words that indicate that we cannot stay where we are. We must move on! However, this is precisely the point where most of us lose our enjoyment of life.

We must learn to seek the next phase in our journey without despising or belittling the place in which we currently find ourselves.

In my own spiritual journey, I finally learned to say, "I'm not where I need to be, but thank God, I'm not where I used to be. I'm okay, and I'm on my way!"

The spiritual struggle that most of us go through would be almost totally alleviated if we understood the principle of enjoying where we are as we move forward in our journey with Christ, making a little more progress each day.

I believe I change daily. I have goals in every area of my life and I desire improvement in all things. This time next year I will be different from what I am now. Various things in my life, family and ministry will have improved. But the good news is that I have discovered the soul-satisfying secret of enjoying where I am on the way to where I am going.

We might say that there is always something new on the horizon. The Lord showed me this truth many years ago as I was considering enrolling in a Bible school program sponsored by our church three evenings a week. It was a major commitment for my husband, Dave, and me. At the time we had three small children at home, and yet we felt God calling us to a new level of ministry. I was excited, but anxious.

Once we made the decision, I began to feel that this commitment would be "the thing" that would make "all" the difference in the world. It seems that we humans are always looking for "it"!

As I was considering this decision, God showed me a horizon. My husband and I were heading toward it, but as we finally came near to it, another horizon appeared out beyond the first one. It represented yet another place to reach for once we had arrived at the current one.

As I pondered what I was seeing, the Lord spoke to my heart and said that there would constantly be new goals out in front of us. I felt like God was telling me not to think in small terms, not to become narrow-minded, not to make small plans, but to always be reaching for the next place that would take me beyond where I was. But while we were taking steps toward the next goal, we could still find joy, peace and fulfillment today, in the *now*. In other words, we could enjoy the journey while we were on the way to where we were going. I regret to say that even though I kept reaching forward and was not complacent, it took several more years before I learned to enjoy each step of the journey.

2

Make a Decision to Enjoy Life

I call heaven and earth to witness this day against
you that I have set before you life and death, the
blessings and the curses; therefore choose life, that
you and your descendants may live.

Deuteronomy 30:19

In the Word of God we are exhorted to choose life. The
Hebrew word translated "life" in Deuteronomy 30:19 is
chay, and means, among other things, "fresh," "strong,"
"lively" and "merry."[1]

In John 10:10, Jesus said that He came that we might
have life. According to *Vine's Expository Dictionary of Biblical Words,* the New Testament Greek word translated "life"
in this verse is *zoe* and means, in part, "...life as God has it,
that which the Father has in Himself, and which He gave to

the Incarnate Son to have in Himself...and which the Son manifested in the world...."[2]

The biblical dictionary then goes on to say, "From this life man has become alienated in consequence of the Fall,... and of this life men become partakers through faith in the Lord Jesus Christ...."

The life being referred to here is not simply a span of time. It is a *quality* of existence—life as God has it. We lost that kind of God-like life due to sin, but we can have it back through Jesus. It is God's gift to us in His Son.

I cannot imagine that God does not lead a thoroughly enjoyable life. To even begin to have an understanding of the quality of life that God enjoys, we must change our modern perspective of what real life really is.

Many people have fallen into the trap of believing that quantity is greater than quality, but this is not true. This lie from Satan has been fuel for the spirit of greed that prevails in our world today. It is becoming more and more difficult to find anything that is of excellent quality. In most industrialized nations of the world, especially in the United States, there is an abundance of everything, and yet there are more unhappy people than ever before.

I believe that if we had more quality and a little less quantity, we would experience more real joy in our everyday lives. It would be far better to live forty years to the fullest, truly enjoying every aspect of life, than to live a hundred years and never enjoy anything. Thank God, we can have both—a long life and a quality life—but I am trying to make a point about quality versus quantity.

As believers, you and I have available to us the same quality of life that God has. His life is not filled with fear, stress, worry, anxiety or depression. God is not impatient, and He is in no hurry. He takes time to enjoy His creation, the works of His hands.

For example, in the account of Creation in Genesis 1, Scripture frequently says that *after* God had created a certain portion of the universe in which we live, He saw that it was good (suitable, pleasant, fitting, admirable), and He approved it. (See verses 4, 10, 12, 18, 21, 25, 31.) It seems to me that if God took the time to enjoy each phase of His creation, His work, then you and I should also take time to enjoy our work. We should work not just to accomplish, but also to enjoy our accomplishments.

Learn to enjoy not only your work and your accomplishments but even the ride to work in the morning. Determine not to get so frustrated about traffic and have your mind on what you need to do when you arrive that you fail to enjoy the trip.

Most people dread and even despise the drive home from work at night. They are tired, traffic is heavy, and they begin to think about all the things they must do, but don't want to do, when they get home—cook dinner, go to the store, cut the grass, change the oil in the car, help the children with homework, etc.

I want to encourage you to be intentional about enjoying every aspect of your day—your time alone in traffic, your time planning for a meeting, your time preparing a meal for your family or whatever it is you need to do.

All it takes to begin to enjoy life to the fullest is a decision.

A Decision Can Change It All!

We will never enjoy life unless we make a quality decision to do so.

In order to live as God intends for us to live, the first thing we must do is truly believe that it is God's will for us to experience continual joy. Then we must decide to enter into that joy. Below is a list of Scripture passages in which Jesus Himself revealed that it is God's will for us to enjoy life.

> **The thief comes only in order to steal and kill and destroy. I came that they may have and enjoy life, and have it in abundance (to the full, till it overflows).**
>
> **John 10:10**

I have told you these things, that My joy and delight may be in you, and that your joy and gladness may be of full measure and complete and overflowing.

John 15:11

Up to this time you have not asked a [single] thing in My Name [as presenting all that I AM]; but now ask and keep on asking and you will receive, so that your joy (gladness, delight) may be full and complete.

John 16:24

And now I am coming to You [Father]; I say these things while I am still in the world, so that My joy may be made full and complete and perfect in them [the disciples] [that they may experience My delight fulfilled in them, that My enjoyment may be perfected in their own souls, that they may have My gladness within them, filling their hearts].

John 17:13

Jesus wants us to experience enjoyment in our souls. It is important to our physical, mental, emotional and spiritual health. Proverbs 17:22 says, **A happy heart is good medicine and a cheerful mind works healing, but a broken spirit dries up the bones.**

It is God's will for us to enjoy life!

As we continue, I will share other insights God has shown me that helped me learn how to have the abundant life Jesus died to give me. Some of them will speak to you, I am sure. Others may not fit your personal situation as well as they did mine, but the principles can be applied anywhere you need them.

"'Relish the moment' is a good motto, especially when coupled with Psalm 118:24 (KJV), **This is the day which the Lord hath made; we will rejoice and be glad in it.**

3

Regret and Dread

I do not consider, brethren, that I have captured
and made it my own [yet]; but one thing I do [it
is my one aspiration]: forgetting what lies behind
and straining forward to what lies ahead,

I press on toward the goal to win the [supreme
and heavenly] prize to which God in Christ Jesus is
calling us upward.

Philippians 3:13-14

Regret of the past and dread of the future are both thieves
of joy.

Let's examine each of them in detail to learn what
causes them and how to avoid them as we continue our
quest to enjoy the abundant life that God has provided for
us through His Son Jesus.

Regret

Many people stay trapped in the past. There is only one thing that can be done about the past: forget it.

When we make mistakes, as we all do, the best thing we can do is ask God's forgiveness and go on. Like Paul says in the verses above, we are all pressing toward the mark of perfection, but none of us has arrived.

I believe Paul enjoyed his life and ministry and this "one aspiration" of his was part of the reason why. Like us, he was pressing toward the mark of perfection, admitting that he had not arrived, but he had insight on how to enjoy his life while he was making the trip.

Until we learn to forget our mistakes and refuse to live in regret of the past, we will never really enjoy life.

Mistakes are a regular part of life, and I spent many years hating myself for each of my failures. I desperately wanted to be a good Christian and please God. But I still thought it was my perfect performance that would please Him. I had not yet learned that He was pleased with my faith.

In Hebrews 11:6, we read, **But without faith it is impossible to please and be satisfactory to Him....**

Even when we make mistakes and waste precious time as a result of those mistakes, being upset when we could be enjoying life, it is useless to continue being miserable for an extended period of time because of the original mistake. Two wrongs never make anything right.

Always remember that regret steals joy *now!*

God has called us to a faith walk. Faith operates in the *now*—at this time.

Hebrews 11:1 states, *Now* **faith is the assurance (the confirmation, the title deed) of the things [we] hope for, being the proof of things [we] do not see and the conviction of their reality [faith perceiving as real fact what is not revealed to the senses].**

This Scripture begins with the word "now." Although I know that the Greek word from which it is translated actually means "but, and, etc.,"[1] rather than "at this point in time," I still believe the term can be used to describe faith itself.

Faith operates *now!*

Without faith, I cannot enjoy my life. Every time I lay aside my faith and stop believing, I lose my peace, and as soon as I lose my peace, my joy goes with it.

There are many things we may find ourselves regretting.

One morning Dave woke me up at the usual time, and I had not had as much sleep as I needed so I decided to sleep a little while longer. I normally get up by 6:00 A.M., but this particular morning I said, "Let me sleep another forty-five minutes."

When Dave woke me up forty-five minutes later, the

first thing I felt and thought was regret that I had not gotten up earlier.

This is the way the devil works. God will tell you what you are about to do wrong, so you can change your mind before you make a mistake. But Satan waits until it's too late, when you can no longer do anything about it, and then tries to bring regret and, ultimately, condemnation upon you.

If it was going to be wrong for me to sleep an additional forty-five minutes, God would have, by His Spirit, made that point clear in my heart before I went back to sleep. He would not have waited until there was nothing I could do about it, and then fill me full of regret so I could not enjoy the rest of my day.

Even if you should oversleep, or go back to bed when in fact you should have been up early, regretting that situation is still not the answer. Repent, ask God to help you use more discipline and self-control the next time and then go on. If you have already wasted part of your day, getting sleep you did not actually need, there is no point in wasting more of it, regretting the part you have already wasted.

You will find many areas in your own life in which Satan tries to cause you regret, which is one of the thieves of joy. Don't let him use regret to steal your enjoyment any longer. Choose to let go of regret and move on to enjoy this day.

Dread

Dread does the same thing to us that regret does, except that dread places us in the future, whereas regret puts us in the past.

I spent a lot of years with regret pulling on one arm and dread pulling on the other. I felt like I was being pulled apart, and I didn't even know what the problem was.

Regret and dread are ruining the lives of many people, stealing their joy in life. And I want to share these truths with you because I believe you can learn from my mistakes and avoid a lot of the misery I endured.

Dreading things can be a habit, an attitude that develops out of lethargy or laziness. Procrastination and dread often work together. An upcoming task is dreaded, so procrastination says, "Put it off until later." That sounds good for a few minutes, but the task is still there to be dreaded until it is finished. It would be far better to do the work and be free to go on to other things.

You may not know it—or realize it—but dread is a close relative of fear.

We know that God has not given us a spirit of fear (2 Tim. 1:7), and since He did not give us fear, we know that He did not give us dread either. As a matter of fact, the Bible teaches us in several places not to dread.

In Deuteronomy 1:29-30, Moses told the Children of Israel not to fear their enemies who had possession of the Promised Land: **Then I said to you, Dread not, neither be afraid of them. The Lord your God Who goes before you, He will fight for you just as He did for you in Egypt before your eyes.**

Notice that verse 30 speaks of "the Lord Who goes before you." Jesus is our Pioneer (Heb. 2:10). That means that He goes out ahead of us and makes a way for us. When a project seems impossible or unpleasant, trust your Pioneer (Jesus) to go ahead of you and pave the way.

I have found that dreading a task is actually more painful than doing it. Once I do it, it is finished; but as long as I put off doing it, the dread lingers on and on.

We may dread something that is major or even something minor. Some people dread getting up in the morning, driving to work, fighting the traffic, facing confrontation, handling the boss or their employees, coming back home after work. They dread washing the dishes, going to the grocery store, doing the laundry, cleaning out the closet, dealing with family members and issues. Some even dread going to bed at night.

In your own life, you may want some new clothes, but dread going shopping. Perhaps you would like to see a friend or relative who lives some distance away, but you don't want to go because you dread the drive. The trip could be made pleasant by a change of attitude. Use the time wisely by praying or listening to audiobooks or sermons.

Most people dread exercise, but it is something we all need. It is important for me to get some kind of aerobic exercise, so I walk on a treadmill. Like most people, I find myself wanting the benefits of exercise, and yet negative thoughts fill my mind and feelings of dread pour over my emotions. However, I do not have to keep these thoughts just because the devil offers them to me. I have learned to say no! As soon as the Holy Spirit makes me aware of the presence of dread, I say,

"No, I'm not going to dread it—I'm just going to do it."

If I let *dread* prevent me from doing my exercise, then I will *regret* that I did not do it. Instead, I use the time I spend exercising in prayer. Sometimes I have my assistant sit with me and we do office business while I exercise.

When exercising, it is possible to listen to your favorite music or even watch television. An adjustment in attitude and approach can change everything.

Let this be a day of decision for you—a day when you decide to no longer operate in regret and dread. Become a *now* person. Live in the present, not the past or the future. God has a plan for your life now. Trust Him today. Don't put it off another day.

Believing God brings you into His rest and puts an end to the torment caused by living in regret and dread, but you must take action to believe God today. Don't wait until tomorrow.

I have learned from experience that living life one day at a time is something that can be done.

God gives me grace for today, but He does not give me grace today for yesterday or tomorrow. When I am in yesterday, it brings great pressure to today. The same thing happens if I am focusing on the future, dreading it or trying to figure it out. I have even discovered that it will make me grouchy, because I have to do it under pressure.

When God anoints something, there is a Holy Spirit ease to it. Oil is one of the symbols of the Holy Spirit, and oil speaks of ease. When that oil or anointing is not there, everything becomes hard.

Without the anointing, things have to be done under pressure. Living in regret and dread is pressure.

Take the pressure off, believe God and enter His rest.

Be a *now* person.

4

Joy and Peace Are Found in Believing

For the kingdom of God is not meat and drink; but righteousness, and peace, and joy in the Holy Ghost.

Romans 14:17 KJV

Joy is never released through unbelief, but it is always present where there is belief.

Believing is so much simpler than not believing.

If we do not believe God, His Word and His promises, then we are left with the labor of reasoning and attempting to work out matters ourselves.

The writer of Hebrews 4:3 noted that **we who have believed (adhered to and trusted in and relied on God),** enter the rest of God. In Hebrews 4:10, he wrote: **For he who has once entered [God's] rest also has ceased from [the weariness and pain] of human labors....**

In Matthew 11:28 Jesus said: **Come to Me, all you who labor and are heavy-laden and overburdened, and I will cause you to rest. [I will ease and relieve and refresh your souls.]**

Jesus instructed us to come to Him, but *how* are we to come to Him? In Hebrews 11:6 we read: **But without faith it is impossible to please and be satisfactory to Him. For whoever would come near to God must [necessarily] believe that God exists and that He is the rewarder of those who earnestly and diligently seek Him [out].** That means that when we come to God, we must do so believing. When we do, we will have joy, and where there is joy, there will also be enjoyment.

"What's the Matter with Me?"

I remember one night when I was very miserable. I was just walking around my house, doing what I needed to do, but I was not happy; I was not enjoying life.

"What's the matter with me, Lord?" I asked. "What is my problem?"

It seemed that something was lurking within me, something that kept draining the joy out of me. As I wandered around the house, I began looking at a Scripture box I kept on my desk.

I flipped it open and the Holy Spirit within me instantly confirmed the Scripture that came up: **May the God of your hope so fill you with all joy and peace in believing [through the experience of your faith] that by the power of the Holy Spirit you may abound and be overflowing (bubbling over) with hope** (Rom. 15:13).

I knew immediately that a large part of my problem was simply that I was doubting instead of believing. I was doubting the call of God on my life, wondering if He would meet our financial need, questioning my decisions and actions, etc.

I had become negative instead of positive.

I was doubting instead of believing.

Doubt is an attitude that can easily creep up on us; however, we can stay spiritually alert by focusing on God's Word and not allow it to determine our mood. Doubt certainly may knock at the door of your heart. When it does, answer with a believing heart, and you will always maintain the victory.

The doubtful, negative mind is filled with reasoning. It rotates around and around the circumstance or situation, attempting to find answers for it. God's Word does not tell us to search for our own answers. We are, however, instructed to trust God with all of our heart and mind, seek Him in all of our ways, and humbly worship Him (Prov.

3:5-7). When we follow the guidelines the Lord has laid out for us, they will bring us His joy and peace.

Joy Defined

God's will for us is that we would have and enjoy life. Jesus did not die for you and me so that we would be miserable. He died to deliver us from every kind of oppression and misery. His work is already finished, and the only thing that remains to be accomplished is for us to *believe.*

Webster defines the word *joy* as "great pleasure or happiness: DELIGHT," "The expression or display of this emotion," "A source or object of pleasure or satisfaction," and (in the archaic form) "To fill with joy," or "To enjoy."[1]

My understanding of joy, resulting from years of studying the subject, is that it covers a wide range of emotions, from calm delight to extreme hilarity. The times of extreme hilarity are fun, and we all need those moments of laughing until our sides hurt. But we probably won't live our lives that way on a day-to-day basis. Later in the book I will discuss the value of laughter. God has given us an ability to laugh, so there must be a reason for it!

We should grow in our ability to enjoy life and be able to say, "I live my life in a state of calm delight." I think calm delight is a mixture of peace and joy.

Celebrate Life

But the fruit of the [Holy] Spirit [the work which His presence within accomplishes] is love, *joy (gladness),* peace, patience (an even temper, forbearance), kindness, goodness (benevolence), faithfulness, gentleness (meekness, humility), self-control (self-restraint, continence)....

Galatians 5:22-23

Doubt and unbelief are thieves of joy, but simple child-like believing releases the joy that is resident in our spirits because of the Holy Spirit Who lives in us. As we see in Galatians 5:22-23, one fruit of the Holy Spirit is joy. Therefore, since we are filled with God's Holy Spirit, we believers should express joy and enjoy our lives.

We can look at it like this: Joy is in the deepest part of the person who has accepted Jesus as Savior—joy is in the believer's spirit. But if our soul (our mind, will and emotions) is filled with worry, negative thoughts, reasoning, doubt and unbelief, these negative things will become like a wall that holds back the release of the fruit of joy living inside of us.

The apostle Peter said to cast all our care (anxieties, worries, concerns) on the Lord (1 Pet. 5:7). Paul exhorted the believers of his day: **Be anxious for nothing, but in everything by** prayer and supplication, *with thanksgiving,* let your requests be made known to God; and the *peace* of God, which surpasses all understanding, will guard your *hearts* and *minds* through Christ Jesus (Phil. 4:6-7 NKJV, emphasis added).

Keep your mind filled with happy, grateful thoughts, and, as you trust God, He will take care of your problems.

God's plan for us is actually so simple that many times we miss it. We tend to look for something more complicated—something more difficult—that we are expected to do to please God. But in John 6:29, Jesus has told us what we are to do to please the Father: "Believe!"

A few years ago, I began to realize that I was a very complicated person and that my habit of complicating things was stealing my joy—it was preventing me from really enjoying life. It was then that God began to speak to me about simplicity.

Frequently, I write in a journal or notebook the things that God is teaching me or dealing with me about. Here are some of the things I wrote when I was really struggling with finding my joy:

"I have been struggling inwardly for a long time with something I cannot even define. I think God is bringing me up out of being complicated and trying to teach me to 'be,' instead of 'do' all the time. He is trying to teach me to enjoy simple things.

"It seems I keep looking for something to do in my free

time that I will really enjoy and I keep coming up with nothing. Tonight, it seems the Lord said to me, 'Learn to enjoy the simple things in life.' And then I wrote, 'God help me. I'm not even sure I know what simplicity is.'"

I have had to learn, and am still learning, what simplicity is and how to approach things with a simple attitude. One of the things I have learned is that *believing is much simpler than doubting.* Doubt brings in confusion and often depression. It causes us to speak doubtful and negative things out of our mouths.

Believing, on the other hand, releases joy and leaves us free to enjoy life while God is taking care of our circumstances and situations. It sounds almost too good to be true, and that is exactly why many people never enter into God's plan. There are countless people who have accepted Jesus as their Savior. They are on their way to heaven, but they are not enjoying the trip.

Living like this is like getting a brand-new house as a gift. You get the keys—to the garage, the front door, the back door, the basement door and all the rooms in the house that have locks on them. The home belongs to you; but you can own it all your life and never live in it and enjoy it if you do not use the keys to open the doors and enter in.

Often the thing that keeps us from entering into and enjoying the life that God has freely bestowed upon us is our own sin consciousness.

Enjoy God

The high call on the life of every believer—the goal each of us should strive for—is to enjoy God. According to John 1:4 and John 14:6, He is Life, and this shows us that we cannot enjoy the life Jesus gives until we learn to enjoy Him.

None of us can enjoy God if we are concerned that He is angry with us most of the time due to our sins.

Jesus came to deliver us from the wrong kind of fear in our relationship with our heavenly Father, and we should be relaxed in His presence. At the same time, we need to have reverential fear, the kind that provokes respect, honor and obedience. But we must cleanse our hearts and minds of any thoughts that the Lord is angry with us. According to His Word, God is full of mercy and compassion and is slow to anger (Neh. 9:17).

A few years ago, the Lord said to me, "Joyce, I am not nearly as hard to get along with as most of you think I am." We are no surprise to God. He knew what He was getting when He drew us into relationship with Himself. We simply need to believe in His love for us.

5
Simplicity

And Jesus answered and said to her, "Martha, Martha, you are worried and troubled about many things. But one thing is needed...."

Luke 10:41-42 NKJV

As I said in the previous chapter, I came to a place in life where I knew that God was dealing with me about simplicity. At the time, I was very complicated in almost everything I did. I could not even entertain friends without complicating it.

Not only were my actions complicated but also my thought processes. I complicated my relationship with the Lord because I had a legalistic approach to righteousness. To me, life itself was complicated. I felt that I had a lot of complex problems, and I didn't realize they were that way only because my approach to life was complicated.

When we are complicated inside, then everything else in life seems that way to us.

Webster defines the word *complicate* as "to make or become complex, intricate, or bewildering," or "to twist or become twisted together."[1] According to this definition, if something is *complicated*, it is "difficult to understand."[2] On the other hand, Webster defines *simple* as "having or composed of only one thing or part," "not complex: EASY," "without additions or modifications," "unassuming or unpretentious," "not deceitful: SINCERE," "having no divisions," "without overtones."[3]

We can learn a lot just from meditating on these definitions. For example: To *complicate* is "to twist together." We can see from that definition that if doubt and unbelief are mixed or twisted together with belief, the result will be complication.

One definition of *complicated* is "bewildering." When I mix doubt and unbelief with belief, I feel bewildered, not knowing what to do, but busily trying to figure it out. I hear so much of this same thing from other believers in Christ who talk with me or ask me for prayer. They are bewildered. Their problems seem to be too much for them. They wonder why their prayers are not heard or answered.

In James 1:6-8, we read that the double-minded (complicated, bewildered) man is unstable in all his ways and that he should not think that he will receive anything he asks from the Lord—and that includes wisdom and guidance.

Whereas something complicated is "complex, intricate and bewildering" and "difficult to understand," anything simple is easy to understand because it is "composed of only one thing."

For years I sought for many things—answers to my situations, prosperity, healing, success in my ministry, changes in my family, etc. Finally, I learned about the "one thing" I was supposed to be seeking.

Centuries ago the psalmist wrote, **One thing have I asked of the Lord, that will I seek, inquire for, and [insistently] require: that I may dwell in the house of the Lord [in His presence] all the days of my life, to behold and gaze upon the beauty [the sweet attractiveness and the delightful loveliness] of the Lord and to meditate, consider, and inquire in His temple** (Ps. 27:4).

I realized that I should have been seeking the "one thing" instead of the many things.

When we seek the Lord, He takes care of all the other things, as Jesus promised in Matthew 6:33: **But seek (aim at and strive after) first of all His [God's] kingdom and His righteousness (His way of doing and being right), and then all these things [you desire and seek after] taken together will be given you besides.**

The account of Mary and Martha also depicts this truth.

Many Things or One Thing?

Now while they were on their way, it occurred that Jesus entered a certain village, and a woman named Martha received and welcomed Him into her house.

And she had a sister named Mary, who seated herself at the Lord's feet and was listening to His teaching.

But Martha [overly occupied and too busy] was distracted with much serving; and she came up to Him and said, Lord, is it nothing to You that my sister has left me to serve alone? Tell her then to help me [to lend a hand and do her part along with me]!

But the Lord replied to her by saying, Martha, Martha, you are anxious and troubled about many things;

There is need of only one or but a few things. Mary has chosen the good portion [that which is to her advantage], which shall not be taken away from her.

Luke 10:38-42

Martha was worried and anxious about many things, but Mary was concerned about only one thing.

Martha was doing what I used to do, running around trying to make everything perfect in order to impress God and everyone else. I used to be concerned about my reputation, about what people thought. I felt better about myself when I was working. I felt that I had worth as long as I was accomplishing something. Like Martha, I resented people like Mary who enjoyed themselves; I thought they should be doing what I was doing.

Now, obviously there is a time to work (John 5:17), and accomplishment is good. The Bible teaches us that we are to bear good, abundant fruit, and when we do, our Father in heaven is glorified (John 15:8). But I was out of balance.

Martha certainly has her place, but so does Mary. My problem was that I was all Martha and no Mary. I loved Jesus, but I had not yet learned about the simple life He desired me to live.

Simplify Your Life!

If you are ever to live simply, you must be determined to gain your freedom from complication and be even more determined to keep it.

2 Corinthians 1:12 KJV is a great Scripture about simplicity, and it connects simplicity and rejoicing: **For our**

rejoicing is this, the testimony of our conscience, that in simplicity and godly sincerity, not with fleshly wisdom, but by the grace of God, we have had our conversation in the world, and more abundantly to you-ward. In this context, the word *conversation* means "conduct" or "behavior."[4]

Here Paul was saying, "We have joy because we have conducted ourselves in simplicity and godly sincerity, not with fleshly wisdom, which always includes a lot of reasoning, but we have lived by the grace of God."

Nothing is more simple than grace.[5]

Simplicity or Complexity?

I used to wonder why there aren't more Scriptures about simplicity, or why the Bible doesn't talk more about it, especially since it seems to be a much needed and sorely abused subject.

The Holy Spirit showed me that the entire New Covenant is simple. It may not frequently use the word "simple," but it is the essence of simplicity, as we see in God's plan of redemption for humanity:

Jesus came and paid for our sins, taking our punishment upon Himself. He became our substitute, paid the debt we owed, at no cost to us. He did all this freely because of His great love, grace and mercy.

He inherited all the Father has to give and tells us that we are joint-heirs with Him by virtue of our faith. He has provided the way for our complete victory both here and hereafter. We are more than conquerors. He has conquered, and we get the reward without the battle.

How much simpler could it be? It is not complicated. We complicate it!

Complication is the work of Satan. When we return to and maintain simplicity, we are warring against him. He hates simplicity, because he knows the power and the joy that it brings.

I also looked for books on simplicity and did not find many of them either. I had to be very open to the Holy Spirit to teach me along the way. Usually, personal experience is the best teacher anyway. I began to systematically watch for times when I had no joy and then ask myself why. Often, I discovered that it was because I was complicating an issue. Here is an example:

Dave and I had an argument one evening close to bedtime. Dave is an easy-going man who has no problem just forgetting things and going on. We said what we both felt that we needed to say, and as far as Dave was concerned, it was over and time to go to bed. He lay down and went right to sleep, and I went into my home office to try to figure out what had happened.

I asked myself: How had we managed to get into an

argument? And, what could I do to be sure it never happened again?

I was determined that I would get an answer, and the longer I stayed up (supposedly seeking God), the more frustrated I became. Finally, about one o'clock in the morning, I said, "Lord, what am I going to do?" He answered and said, "Why not simply go to bed?"

Here is another example:

Entertaining friends and guests in our home was something I wanted to do, but never really enjoyed in the end. As I opened my heart to God, He began to show me that I made a project out of entertaining. I could make plans for a simple barbecue with three other couples, and, before it was over, I would turn the simple plans into a nightmare.

Much complication is born out of an ungodly need to impress people.

I was abused in my childhood and, as a result, I was very insecure about myself. People who are insecure normally strive to impress others because they feel they are not very impressive just being who they are.

When I entertained, everything had to be perfect—just the right food and drinks, the house had to look immaculate, the yard manicured and all the lawn furniture spotless. All the children had to look like they just stepped out of a fashion magazine, and, of course, I had to have on just the right outfit, and every single hair had to be in place.

I worked so hard outwardly and inwardly before the event started that I was worn-out by the time our guests arrived. Even their arrival did not put an end to my labor. I continued to work most of the time they were there—setting food out and putting food away, washing dishes and sweeping the kitchen floor so none of the crumbs would get tracked onto my carpets.

Then I would have resentment in my heart and quite often in my mouth, because it seemed that everyone else had fun and enjoyed themselves, and all I did was work.

Finally, I had to face the truth that I was creating the problem. I could have taken a much simpler approach. I could have grilled some hot dogs and hamburgers, heated up some baked beans and set out a bowl of potato chips.

I didn't have to buy steaks that we couldn't afford, make potato salad that was a two-hour project and fix enough other side dishes to feed a small army. (I always wanted to make sure we never ran out of food so I always made way too much.) I could have made iced tea, coffee and lemonade, but I had to have all that plus four kinds of soda pop.

I hope you're getting the picture that in order for my life to be simpler so it could be enjoyed, I had to change. Life was not going to change; I had to change.

I imagine it will be the same way with you. I suggest that you start to look for all the ways that you complicate things and ask the Holy Spirit to teach you to keep it simple.

Simple Prayer

My prayer life was another area that I struggled with, and I discovered that much of it was due to a complicated approach.

First of all, I had listened to too much of what everyone else said I should be praying about. Most people are full of what God has called them to do and what He has anointed them for, and without even meaning to do harm, they get on their personal soapbox, so to speak, and attempt to get everyone doing what they are doing.

I was as guilty as anyone else in this area, until God got the point across to me that I have to do what I am anointed to do and let everyone else do what He has anointed them to do.

People told me I should pray about government issues—that the government was in such a mess and really needed a lot of prayer. Others said I should pray about abortion, AIDS or the homeless. Missionaries told me that it was missions I should be praying about. Some said I should do spiritual warfare, others said to confess the Word.

I heard people teach on prayer, and it seemed I always came out of those meetings with one more thing I needed to do while praying. People told me how long to pray—it should be at least one hour. People who were early risers told me it was better to get up and pray early in the morning.

Let me say that we will find ourselves praying about all

of these issues and for the correct amount of time and at the right time of day for us, *if* we follow the leading of the Holy Spirit in prayer.

I had turned all of my "instructions" from people into laws—things I felt I *had* to pray about. (If you have a complicated approach to the Word of God, it will all become laws instead of promises.) I finally cried out to God and asked Him to teach me to pray, and He taught me some wonderful things that have brought the joy into prayer that is supposed to be there.

First of all, the Lord taught me that I had to pray for what He put on my heart, not for what everyone else wanted to put on my heart. He showed me that I had to pray when He was prompting and leading, for the length of time He put the desire in my heart to do it. He made me see that I would never enjoy prayer if I was in the lead; I had to allow Him to lead me.

The Lord also taught me that I should approach Him simply. This is a very important point. Like any good father, God wants His beloved children to approach Him simply and gently. Somehow I had gotten into doing a lot of yelling in prayer, and although there may be a time for an aggressive tone of voice, I was way out of balance.

I learned that I didn't have to repeat words and phrases over and over, which we have a tendency to do in order to make our prayers sound impressive. Why can't we learn to simply state our need, ask for God's gracious help and go on to the next thing?

The Lord showed me that instead of praying loud and long, I was to say what was on my heart and believe that He heard me, and that He would take care of it His way, in His timing.

As a result of what I learned from the Lord about praying, I developed my faith in what I call "the simple prayer of faith," as described in James 5:13-15:

> **Is anyone among you afflicted (ill-treated, suffering evil)? He should pray. Is anyone glad at heart? He should sing praise [to God].**
>
> **Is anyone among you sick? He should call in the church elders (the spiritual guides). And they should pray over him, anointing him with oil in the Lord's name.**
>
> **And the prayer [that is] of faith will save him who is sick, and the Lord will restore him; and if he has committed sins, he will be forgiven.**

Sometimes when I simply present to God my need or the need of another individual, it seems in my "natural man" that I should do or say more. I have found that when I pray what the Holy Spirit is giving me, without adding to it out of my own flesh, the prayer is very simple and not exceedingly long.

My mind wants to say, "Well, that's not enough." Our flesh generally wants to go beyond what the Spirit is giving us, and that's when we are robbed of the enjoyment that each thing is supposed to bring.

Let us say that a parent comes to me and asks me to pray for a difficult child. I say, "Father, we come to You in the name of Jesus. I am placing a prayer cover over this family. I ask You to bring them back together. Bring unity between this parent and this child. Whatever the problem is, Father, I ask You to remove the things that need to be removed, and to bring forth the things that need to be brought forth. Amen!"

This kind of prayer is short and simple and really says everything that needs to be said, but the flesh wants to add to it. The carnal mind says, "It's not long enough—not eloquent enough." It required real discipline on my part to go as far as the Holy Spirit was going and no further. Keep prayer simple, and you will enjoy it more.

The Simple Approach

Remembering the definition of *simple* as "easy," let's take a look again at Jesus' words as recorded in Matthew 11:28-30. I would like for you to notice how often the words "ease" and "easy" appear in this passage:

Come to Me, all you who labor and are heavy-laden and overburdened, and I will cause you to rest. [I will *ease* and relieve and refresh your souls.]

Take My yoke upon you and learn of Me, for I am gentle (meek) and humble (lowly) in heart, and you will find rest (relief and *ease* and refreshment and recreation and blessed quiet) for your souls.

For My yoke is wholesome (useful, good—not harsh, hard, sharp, or pressing, but comfortable, gracious, and pleasant), and My burden is light and *easy* to be borne.

First of all, Jesus said, "Learn of Me." I believe He meant, "Learn how I handle situations and people. Learn what My response would be to any given circumstance, and follow My ways."

Jesus was not stressed-out or burned-out. He was not controlled by circumstances and by the demands of other people.

In John 14:6 He said, **I am the Way.** His way is the right way—the way that will lead us into righteousness, peace and joy. Remember that in John 15:11, He prayed that His enjoyment would fill our souls. That is not going to happen unless we learn a different approach to life and its many different circumstances.

When you're facing a problem, ask yourself, "What

would Jesus do in this situation?" You will find many times that you are trying to handle something Jesus would leave alone. Sometimes when I want to confront an issue, I will hear the Lord say, "Leave it alone."

On the other hand, there will be times when you want to leave something alone and not deal with it, but when you listen to your heart, you know that you need to handle it before it grows into a worse mess.

Sometimes you will want to be part of something exciting that is going on, and God will tell you no. Other times, you may prefer not to be involved, and yet the Lord will say, "I need you in this."

You and I will not always know the "why" behind all of the Holy Spirit's leadings, but simplicity obeys promptly. It is complicated to disobey and have a guilty conscience. Disobedience truly steals the enjoyment of life.

God may tell you no about something at one time, and then at another time allow you to do it. There are no rules except to follow the Word of God and the Spirit of God.

Simplicity and Decisions

But above all [things], my brethren, do not swear, either by heaven or by earth or by any other oath; but let your yes be [a simple] yes, and your no be

[a simple] no, so that you may not sin and fall
under condemnation.

James 5:12

My husband does not mind shopping with me at all,
which is a blessing because most men do not enjoy shopping. He gives me a reasonable amount of time to make my
choices, but if I go back and forth too many times, he starts
wanting to leave.

He says, "Do something. I don't mind being here if we
are making progress, but just wandering around and never
making any choice is a waste of time."

That does not mean that it is wrong to take a certain
amount of time to look things over and search for a good bar-
gain, but if looking and searching go too far, decision-making
becomes complicated. Keep it simple. Buy something and
move on to the next thing.

I can really get into doublemindedness when I am shopping for other people. I normally feel that I know what I
like, but I am not sure about others. Often I search for the
"perfect" gift to the point of losing valuable time. I have
done that with my children. And even after all my special
effort, they returned what I bought for them.

Whatever the problem or situation, making a decision is
always better than wavering between doubt and indecision.
So once again, keep it simple. You will see your joy increase.

6

Childlikeness

And He [Jesus] called a little child to Himself and put him in the midst of them,

And said, Truly I say to you, unless you repent (change, turn about) and become like little children [trusting, lowly, loving, forgiving], you can never enter the kingdom of heaven [at all].

Whoever will humble himself therefore and become like this little child [trusting, lowly, loving, forgiving] is greatest in the kingdom of heaven.

Matthew 18:2-4

In Luke 18:17, Jesus expressed this same message about the spiritual importance of being childlike when He said, **Truly I say to you, whoever does not accept and receive and welcome the kingdom of God like a little child [does] shall not in any way enter it [at all].**

As we see, *The Amplified Bible* translation of Matthew 18:3 states that the defining attributes of a child are:

trusting, lowly, loving and forgiving. Oh, how much more we would enjoy our lives if we operated in those four virtues.

Children believe what they are told. Some people say children are gullible, meaning they believe anything no matter how ridiculous it sounds. But children are not gullible, they are trusting. *It is a child's nature to trust* unless that child has experienced something that teaches him or her otherwise.

One thing we all know about children is that they enjoy life. A child can literally enjoy anything, and even turn work into a game in order to enjoy it.

I recall asking my son to sweep the patio when he was about eleven or twelve years old. I looked outside and saw him dancing with the broom to the music playing on the headset he was wearing.

I thought, *"Amazing!* He has turned sweeping into a game. If he had to do it—he was going to enjoy it."

We should all have that attitude. We may not choose to dance with a broom, but we should choose an attitude that allows us to enjoy all aspects of life.

The Child in All of Us

All healthy adults should also have a child inside of them. Each of us starts out in life as a child, and as we grow up, we need to protect that child within us.

Satan is always out to kill the child. He put it in Herod's heart to issue an order that every male child in Bethlehem two years old and under be put to death. Because Herod was frightened of the newborn Christ Child, the King of the Jews, whom the wise men had come from the east to see and worship, he wanted to get rid of Him (Matt. 2:1-16).

I find it interesting that Satan was afraid of a child, and that a child was the King of the Jews. Kings rule, and perhaps the lesson here, at least in part, is that if we desire to rule and reign as kings in life (Rom. 5:17; Rev. 1:6), we must also become like little children. When we become childlike, it frightens the devil just as the Christ Child frightened Herod.

From Revelation 12:4-5, we can see how Satan seeks to devour the child from birth:

His tail swept [across the sky] and dragged down a third of the stars and flung them to the earth. And the dragon stationed himself in front of the woman who was about to be delivered, so that he might devour her child as soon as she brought it forth.

And she brought forth a male Child, One Who is destined to shepherd (rule) all the nations with an iron staff (scepter), and her Child was caught up to God and to His throne.

Of course, these Scriptures are referring to Jesus, but I believe there is a principle here from which we may learn.

Like many people, I was abused in my childhood. Satan did not wait until I was an adult to try to destroy me—he started early.

Children are not able to protect and defend themselves. And Satan, acting as a bully, often attacks those who seem powerless to fight back. The devil desired to destroy me, mentally and emotionally, as well as to prevent me from ever fulfilling God's plan for my life. He stole my childhood through sexual, verbal, mental and emotional abuse.

I grew up in a dysfunctional home where alcoholism, violence and incest were prevalent. I did not like being a child. As a matter of fact, I hated it. To me, childhood meant being pushed around, taken advantage of, controlled and used. I was very anxious to grow up—it was my predominant thought. I lay in bed many nights and thought about how it would be when I was an adult and nobody could control me.

My plan was to grow up and never allow anyone to hurt me ever again. Of course, this meant that I could not trust anyone, and I had to take care of myself. I did not have the character attributes we listed for a child—trusting, lowly, loving and forgiving. I also had no joy or enjoyment of anything. I occasionally had fun, but never knew any real joy.

I became a workaholic and was driven by the need to

succeed. I carried a false sense of responsibility that never allowed me to enjoy anything. I did not know how to do my part and allow others to do theirs. Nor did I know how to let God do His part by trusting Him.

Because of my insecurities, coupled with a determination never to "need" anyone, work became an idol for me. It made me feel that I had worth. I thought God would bless me if I worked really hard.

The Bible does say that as His beloved children, God will bless us in all that we undertake (Deut. 28:8). But we are never to derive our sense of worth and value from what we do. We should know who we are in Christ Jesus, and our work should have value because *we* do it, not the other way around.

In his book *The Rhythm of Life,* Richard Exley wrote, "There is not enough success in the world to quiet the discordant voices within. Self-esteem is not the by-product of achievement, but the natural consequence of a healthy relationship with one's parents, peers, and, of course, God. It is a matter of who you are, not what you have done."[1]

Work is necessary, and it is good, but if it is exalted to a place in our lives that it was never meant to have, then the good thing becomes our enemy. And we can then think the enemy is our friend.

I thought work was my best friend. It gave me a feeling of "belonging," as I said previously—a feeling of worth and value. Actually, it was my enemy because I was out of balance.

In *The Amplified Bible* version of 1 Peter 5:8, the apostle warned, **Be well balanced (temperate, sober of mind), be vigilant and cautious at all times; for that enemy of yours, the devil, roams around like a lion roaring [in fierce hunger], seeking someone to seize upon and devour.**

Areas that are out of balance in our lives are open doors for the enemy. He stalks around looking for these doors. We Christians are often busy fighting demons when what we actually need is the restoration of a balanced life.

In my own case, I needed to work, but I also needed to play; however, I saw no value in play. I actually did not even know how to properly enter into play as an adult, and truly enjoy it. Even when I did fun things, I always had a vague feeling that I really should be working. I actually felt guilty when I tried to relax or enjoy myself.

Thankfully, as God has brought healing and restoration to my soul, I've learned how to be balanced with my time and priorities. Now I'm able to purposely enjoy everything I do, and I'm free to enjoy the life Jesus has given me.

I believe one of the ways we maintain our liberty is through frequent reminders of who we are in Christ.

I have noticed that Jesus referred to His disciples at times as "little children." In John 21:1-6, we read about a situation in which Peter and some of the other disciples decided to go fishing and had an unexpected encounter with the risen Christ:

After this, Jesus let Himself be seen and revealed [Himself] again to the disciples, at the Sea of Tiberias. And He did it in this way:

There were together Simon Peter, and Thomas, called the Twin, and Nathanael from Cana of Galilee, also the sons of Zebedee, and two others of His disciples.

Simon Peter said to them, I am going fishing! They said to him, And we are coming with you! So they went out and got into the boat, and throughout that night they caught nothing.

Morning was already breaking when Jesus came to the beach and stood there. However, the disciples did not know that it was Jesus.

So Jesus said to them, Boys (children), you do not have any meat (fish), do you? [Have you caught anything to eat along with your bread?] They answered Him, No!

And He said to them, Cast the net on the right side of the boat and you will find [some]. So they cast the net, and now they were not able to haul it in for such a big catch (mass, quantity) of fish [was in it].

It seems to me that in deciding to jump up and go fishing, these disciples quickly made an emotional decision that did not produce the desired result. We also frequently make fleshly emotional decisions that do not produce anything until we learn that apart from Jesus we can do nothing (John 15:5).

Jesus came to the beach and addressed them in this manner:... **Boys** *(children),* **you do not have any meat (fish), do you? [Have you caught anything to eat along with your bread?]** ... (John 21:5, emphasis mine).

Perhaps Jesus was using this terminology to remind them of their need to come as little children and totally depend on Him.

We see the apostle John using the same phrase in 1 John 2:1: **My** *little children,* **I write you these things so that you may not violate God's law and sin. But if anyone should sin, we have an Advocate (One Who will intercede for us) with the Father—[it is] Jesus Christ [the all] righteous [upright, just, Who conforms to the Father's will in every purpose, thought, and action].** He also used this term in 1 John 2:12: **I am writing to you,** *little children,* **because for His name's sake your sins are forgiven [pardoned through His name and on account of confessing His name].**

Perhaps John learned this expression from hearing Jesus refer to him and the other disciples in this way. It seems to be endearing terminology that immediately puts us at rest, makes us feel loved and cared for and lets us know that we need to lean on the Lord for everything.

If I were to call my son "baby" all the time, it would put an attitude in his mind (even in his subconscious) that I saw him as a baby, and it might even develop in him an attitude of immaturity. I noticed myself calling my boys "son" as they got older. I believe the change of name helped them grow up. They knew I was expecting some maturity from them just because of what I called them.

There are also times when I tell all four of our children that no matter how old they get, they will always be my babies. They know from this that they can depend on us to help them in a balanced way any time they need it. They can always come to us if they are hurting.

Jesus wants us to grow up in our behavior, but He also wants us to remain childlike in our attitude toward Him concerning trust and dependence. He knows that we cannot have peace and enjoy life unless we do so.

We Are God's Children

[And the Lord answered] Can a woman forget her nursing child, that she should not have compassion on the son of her womb? Yes, they may forget, yet I will not forget you.

Isaiah 49:15

Isaiah 49:15 is another Scripture that reveals that our heavenly Father desires us to come to Him as children. In this verse, the Lord uses the example of a nursing mother and how she tenderly cares for and has compassion on her child and his needs.

Our heavenly Father wants us to know that we are His precious little ones—His children—and that when we come to Him as such, we show faith in Him, which releases Him to care for us.

God is not like people. If people in your past have hurt you, don't let it affect your relationship with the Lord. You can trust Him. He will care for you as a loving Father.

When we do not receive the care and love that we should in our childhood, it causes fears that were never in God's plan for us. Parents are to be a mirror image in the physical realm of what our relationship with God is to be like in the spiritual realm. Frequently, when individuals are reared in dysfunctional homes, it causes problems in their relationship with the Lord.

I pray that as you read these words and meditate on the Scriptures I am sharing, you will experience healing in your emotions that will set you free to be a responsible adult who can come to your heavenly Father in a childlike way—an adult who knows how to work hard when it is time to work, and how to play freely when it is time to play—one who can maintain godly balance in being serious and having fun.

We must come to God as little children or we will never walk in obedience (1 Peter 1:14). We must lean on Him and continually ask for His help. Everything that God has called us to do, He must help us do. He is ready, waiting, and more than willing. But we must come humbly as little children—sincere, unpretentious, honest, open—knowing that without Him and His continual help, we will never walk in new levels of obedience.

In 1 John 4:4 the apostle wrote, **Little children, you are of God [you belong to Him] and have [already] defeated and overcome them [the agents of the antichrist], because He Who lives in you is greater (mightier) than he who is in the world.**

The Greek word translated *children* in this verse, as well as many others, is partially defined as "darlings."[2] God wants you and me to know that we are His little darlings.

In 1 John 4:4 the apostle speaks of defeating and overcoming the enemy. Once again, I believe we need to see that this is only accomplished as we come to God as little children—leaning, depending, relying, trusting, etc.

In Galatians 4:19, the apostle Paul called the believers in Galatia, **My little children, for whom I am again suffering birth pangs until Christ is completely and permanently formed (molded) within you.**

Just as loving parents are willing to suffer for their children if need be, Paul was suffering persecution in order to preach the Gospel to those he called his children. They were ones who had been born into the Kingdom of God through Paul's preaching, and he longed to see them grow up and enjoy all that Jesus died to give them.

In referring to them as children, Paul was letting them know that he was ready to stand by them and do whatever was necessary, including suffering if need be, in order to see God's purpose accomplished in their lives.

Good parents would rather suffer themselves than see their children suffer. We see this "parenting principle" in operation when the Father sent Jesus to die for us, His children.

7

The Complication of Religion

**But to as many as did receive and welcome Him
[Jesus], He gave the authority (power, privilege, right)
to become the children of God, that is, to those who
believe in (adhere to, trust in, and rely on) His name.**

John 1:12

Jesus has invited us to be in relationship—through Him—with God, the Father. Relationship and religion are entirely different things.

In society today the question is often asked, "What religion are you?" meaning, "What set of doctrines do you follow?" or, "What set of rules do you adhere to?"

When I am asked that question, I usually respond this way: "I am a member of a non-denominational church, but I am not religious. I have a personal relationship with Jesus Christ." Of course, I get some strange looks as a result of my answer.

Let's examine these two concepts of religion and relationship to see the important difference between them.

Religion

A portion of Webster's definition of *religion* is as follows: "Belief in and reverence for a supernatural power accepted as the creator and governor of the universe...A specific unified system of this expression."[1] Religion does not seem to be a very personal thing. There is nothing warm about the meaning of this word.

Here, religion is described as a "system." I don't want a system. The world does not need a system; we need what Jesus died to give us—we need *life*. Religion does not minister life to us—it ministers death.

Religion is complicated. There is nothing simple about it! Religion focuses on what *we* can do to follow the system—the rules—in order to gain God's favor.

A woman attending one of my conferences once shared with me the definition she felt God had given her for religion: "Religion is man's idea of God's expectations."

The Pharisees in the Bible were religious. In fact, they were the religious elite of their day, and Jesus called them vipers (Matt. 12:34) and whitewashed tombs (Matt. 23:27). Based on this description, religion is not something we should seek.

Relationship

Webster defines *relationship* as "the state or fact of being related... Connection by blood or marriage: KINSHIP."[2]

I already like the word "relationship" better than "religion" without even going any further. Just reading the definition of relationship makes me feel better. It sounds warmer and friendlier and has more life for me than what I read about religion.

In Ezekiel 36:26-28, God promised that the day would come when He would give people His heart, put His Spirit in them, cause them to walk in His statutes and bring them into a new relationship with Him:

> A new heart will I give you and a new spirit will I put within you, and I will take away the stony heart out of your flesh and give you a heart of flesh.
>
> And I will put my Spirit within you and cause you to walk in My statutes, and you shall heed My ordinances and do them.
>
> And you shall dwell in the land that I gave to your fathers; and you shall be My people, and I will be your God.

We are now living in a time when the fulfillment of that promise is available to us.

The Lord said that He would take away the stony heart

out of man. The Law was given on tablets of stone, and I believe that laboring for years trying to keep the Law—and failing—will give anyone a hard, stony heart.

Legalism makes us hardhearted.

Trying, failing, and continually being disappointed leaves us as cold and lifeless as stone, as Paul noted in Galatians 3:10: **And all who depend on the Law [who are seeking to be justified by obedience to the Law of rituals] are under a curse and doomed to disappointment and destruction....**

The Lord has promised that we will be able to keep His statutes because He will give us a heart to do so, and His Spirit to make us able.

The born-again believer does not have to "try" to follow God's ways; he wants to—he desires to. His motives are right.

My response to Jesus is motivated by what He has already done for me—it's not an effort to get Him to do something. I'm not trying to please God to get Him to love me; His love is a free gift that I have received. I want to please God *because* I love Him. That's the difference between having religion versus relationship with God.

Grace Versus Law

But now the righteousness of God has been revealed independently and altogether apart from

the Law, although actually it is attested by the Law and the Prophets,

Namely, the righteousness of God which comes by believing with personal trust and confident reliance on Jesus Christ (the Messiah). [And it is meant] for all who believe. For there is no distinction,

Since all have sinned and are falling short of the honor and glory which God bestows and receives.

[All] are justified and made upright and in right standing with God, freely and gratuitously by His grace (His unmerited favor and mercy), through the redemption which is [provided] in Christ Jesus,

Whom God put forward [before the eyes of all] as a mercy seat and propitiation by His blood [the cleansing and life-giving sacrifice of atonement and reconciliation, to be received] through faith. This was to show God's righteousness, because in His divine forbearance He had passed over and ignored former sins without punishment.

It was to demonstrate and prove at the present time (in the now season) that He Himself is righteous and that He justifies and accepts as righteous him who has [true] faith in Jesus.

Romans 3:21-26

The apostle Paul had his work cut out for him when he was given the task of preaching grace to the Jewish people of his day. They had been trying to keep the Law for a long time. For centuries they had lived under "the system." When they succeeded, they felt good about themselves, and when they failed, they felt condemned.

As Paul expounded here in Romans 3:21-26, they were having a difficult time understanding the new order of things, so he had to teach them about God's grace which justifies and accepts as righteous all those who have faith in Jesus Christ, Who is Himself the fulfillment of the Law.

After Paul preached this message to the Jews, which is amazingly good news, he told them something that, to the religious person, is not good news.

Faith Versus Works

Then what becomes of [our] pride and [our] boasting? It is excluded (banished, ruled out entirely). On what principle? [On the principle] of doing good deeds? No, but on the principle of faith.

For we hold that a man is justified and made upright by faith independent of and distinctly apart from good deeds (works of the Law). [The observance of the Law has nothing to do with justification.]

Romans 3:27-28

As humans, we want to have something to feel proud about. We want to take credit for making ourselves good. In God's new plan, there never would be, and could never be, any credit given to humans. Jesus has done everything that is needed for us to be made right with God, and all we are to do is believe!

Everything that we receive from God is attained by faith, not by works.

First we have to have faith, and then we can certainly do good works, but we need to always bear in mind that those "works" do not earn us any particular favor with God. We are to do them from a pure heart motive, which is a desire to give, not to get!

Believers in Christ should be bubbling over with *life.* It should be vibrant, alive, active, energized, peaceful and joy-filled. I believe with all my heart, as a result of my own experience—in addition to what I have watched other people go through—that a wrong approach to God will totally prevent this kind of vitalized living.

A legalistic, religious approach steals life. It does not nourish it. Remember, Paul said, "The Law kills, but the

Spirit makes alive" (2 Cor. 3:6). When we follow the Spirit, we feel alive. When we follow the Law, it drains the life out of us.

The Church of Jesus Christ is supposed to be glorious (Eph. 5:27 kjv). Remember, of course, that the Church is made up of individual members. Each of us should ask the question, "Would people want what I have by watching my life and seeing my attitude?" We are to be the light of the world (Matt. 5:14), enjoying the abundant life Jesus came to give us, to the full, till it overflows! (John 10:10)

8

Legalism in Practical Matters

I bear them witness that they have a [certain] zeal and enthusiasm for God, but it is not enlightened and according to [correct and vital] knowledge.

Romans 10:2

A legalistic approach affects every area of life.

I used to be legalistic about my housework. I cleaned our entire home every day. I vacuumed, dusted, buffed the hardwood floor, shined the mirrors, and washed, dried, and folded whatever laundry had accumulated from the previous day. I had no time to do anything except work, and I resented the fact that I never seemed to have any enjoyment. Without realizing it, I was robbing myself of the enjoyment I so desperately wanted but could not seem to find in my life.

One day some of my friends invited me to go shopping

with them. I wanted to go. My heart said, "Yes, go have a good time," but my flesh said, "No, work before fun!"

I was walking down the hall, getting ready to start cleaning, when the Holy Spirit spoke to my heart: "Joyce, this dirt will still be here tomorrow. The work will wait for you. Sometimes you have to walk away from it and have a little diversion. I call it the spice in life. Eating bland food will keep you from dying, but it is so much better when it is flavored with a little spice."

A workaholic—which is what I was—gets the job done. Workaholics may even gain the admiration of their peers, but workaholics usually don't enjoy life very much. Also, they frequently start showing signs of the stress under which they live. Stress shows up on their faces, in their bodies, in their emotions and even in their minds.

"Workaholism" puts a burden on the entire family, and sometimes it places so much stress on a marriage that it ends in divorce.

Occasionally, we see a "worker" who is married to a person with a fun-loving personality. God brings such opposite marriage partners together to help them maintain balance in their lives. The fun-loving person may need to learn to work a little more, and the worker may need to learn to have more fun.

God's design is that we learn from each other and help to strengthen or cover one another's weaknesses. We are to keep each other balanced. By watching other people, we may realize that we are out of balance in one area or another.

When a workaholic marries, he may realize that everyone does not love work the way he does. In my case, I was always trying to get Dave to get up and work. He worked all week as an engineer, and on the weekends he enjoyed watching a ball game, going to the golf course or playing with the children. I would nag him to do something "worthwhile." I actually saw no value in enjoyment. I wanted it, but was afraid of it.

In all fairness I must say that I like work, and I am not ashamed to admit it. I am a worker; God fashioned me that way. If He hadn't, this book would not have been written. It requires a lot of hard work to do anything worthwhile, but the good news is that now I also like enjoyment. I have learned to leave my work and enjoy the "spice" in life anytime I feel like things are getting "bland."

Dave was a hard worker, but he managed to enjoy everything he did. I can truly say that my husband has always "celebrated" life. He didn't mind going to the grocery store with me and the children. But if he went, he was going to have a good time. He chased the kids around the store with the grocery cart while they screamed, laughed and yelled with delight.

Of course, his behavior just irritated me. I would tell

him repeatedly, "Will you stop it! People are staring at us. You're making a scene!" But none of it stopped him. If anything, it spurred him on. He occasionally chased me with the grocery cart, which really upset me!

Dave is six feet, five inches tall, and he is able to see over the tops of the grocery aisles. He would get in the aisle next to me, and, of course, he could see me, but I couldn't see him. He would throw things over the aisle at me, leaving me wondering what in the world was going on.

I was a very intense person. I did everything with extreme concentration. Going to the grocery store was a major project for me. At the time, we only had seventy dollars for groceries every two weeks and a family of five to feed. I was a coupon clipper, so I always had my calculator and box of coupons with me.

In addition, I was health conscious, so I spent a lot of time in the store reading labels to be sure I was not giving my family things that were loaded with sugar or other harmful things.

One day I was extra frustrated with Dave. I was yelling at him, and he finally said, "For crying out loud, Joyce, I'm just trying to have a little fun!" To which I responded, "I did not come here to have fun!" And the sad thing was I didn't do anything to have fun.

As I look back now, it is obvious why I was unhappy, but at the time, I was deceived and didn't even know it. I just thought everyone else who did not behave according to my standards was lazy or frivolous. As a result, I wouldn't permit myself to enjoy anything.

But over time, as I pursued a deeper, more intimate relationship with God through Bible study and prayer, the Holy Spirit gave me this revelation: *I was my own worst enemy because I didn't believe I should enjoy anything unless I deserved it.* And no matter how hard I tried each day, I never hit the mark of "perfection," so I always felt vaguely guilty about enjoying my life.

It's so wonderful to know that God's plan is for us to experience His peace and joy in *every area* of our lives— even the practical matters of everyday life.

We are on the earth, and there are earthly things that we must tend to. We cannot be "spiritual" all the time. But if any person has what I call a "religious spirit" about him, he will either ignore the natural things he should be taking care of and create a major problem in his life, or if he does take care of the earthly or secular things, he will not enjoy them.

He will always be rushing through those mundane things, trying to get back to some spiritual activity, because it is only then that he feels good about himself. He only feels approved by God when he is doing what he thinks are "spiritual" things.

We must learn that we can communicate with God while doing the laundry as well as on bended knee. I personally believe God prefers to talk with us intermittently throughout the day, rather than just during a scheduled time that we have for prayer. We can have ongoing communication with God all day long, no matter what we're doing.

The Lord is always with us, and He's always ready to interact with us or to help us with our needs.

It's very important that we have a daily time set aside to spend with God in prayer and Bible study. My point here is that in order to enjoy my entire life, I had to learn that He wants to be involved in everything I do.

God's Presence Makes the Place Holy

And Moses said, I will now turn aside and see this great sight, why the bush is not burned.

And when the Lord saw that he turned aside to see, God called to him out of the midst of the bush and said, Moses, Moses! And he said, Here am I.

God said, Do not come near; put your shoes off your feet, for *the place on which you stand is holy ground.*

Exodus 3:3-5

God called me into ministry while I was in my bedroom making my bed and talking with Him. Making a bed is a rather mundane thing. There isn't anything particularly spiritual or exciting about it, yet God chose to speak to me about taking a direction that would greatly alter the entire course of my life and my family's lives while I was in my home engaged in this very ordinary, everyday activity.

If we will let Him into every area of our lives, we will be amazed at the times and places the Lord will speak to us.

When God appeared to Moses at the burning bush, He told him to take his sandals off his feet because the place on which he was standing was holy ground. A few seconds before God showed up, it was ordinary ground—now it had become holy ground. His presence made it holy! And His presence is in the believer who has accepted Jesus Christ as Savior.

We are God's tabernacle; our bodies are the temple of the Holy Spirit (1 Cor. 6:19). He lives in us! Wherever we go, He goes. If we go to the grocery store, He goes. If we go play golf, He goes. If we go to the park with our children, He goes.

All these ordinary things are things we either must do, or should do, to maintain balance in our lives. The things we do and the places we go in our everyday lives are not holy in themselves, but when we go there and do them, God has promised to be with us. And any place God is becomes holy.

Secular things can become sacred things when the Lord

is present. If you and I do all that we do for the honor and glory of God, then it can all be done with an awareness of His presence—we can "do life" with God!

Life in Christ is so wonderful, and I believe we should celebrate every aspect of it. Webster defines the word *celebrate* in part as "to observe an occasion with...festivity."[1] Life is certainly a special occasion and should be celebrated with festivities, especially a festive attitude. Our daily confession should be Psalm 118:24 KJV: **This is the day which the Lord hath made; we will rejoice and be glad in it.**

Enjoy Life!

Learning to enjoy every part of our lives—both spiritual and practical—is important because if we are not careful, we will become so spiritually minded we won't be any earthly good. We read about the great men and women of God in the Bible and Church history who did great exploits. If we are not on our guard, we may begin to feel that unless we are doing great exploits, nothing we are doing is worthwhile.

But we must remember that those people did not do great exploits day in and day out. We hear about the great things they accomplished through their faith in God, but they had a natural, practical side to their lives also. They got up in the morning with bad breath just like the rest of us. They had to make a living and deal with unpleasant people. They had to clean house, get along with their spouses and take care of their children. And they had to learn to maintain balance; otherwise, books would not have been written about them, because people who are not living balanced, disciplined lives as they are led by the Holy Spirit don't do great exploits for God.

When I say that we should enjoy ourselves, I am not promoting carnality. I simply mean that we should enjoy *all* of life.

How many people raise children but never take time to enjoy them? How many millions of people are married and do not really enjoy their spouse?

Learn to enjoy people. Enjoy your spouse, your family and your friends. Learn to enjoy your own unique personality and individuality, rather than being critical of yourself.

Enjoy your home. Enjoy some of your money *now*. Don't make the mistake of always looking ahead to retirement, thinking that's when you will do all the things you always wanted to do in life.

The bottom line is there is a practical side to life. If we live it with a legalistic, rigid mindset, it will not be enjoyable. Jesus came that we might have life and enjoy it to the full, until it overflows. Do your best to fulfill His purpose and plan by enjoying the practical matters in your life.

9
Too Many Problems to Enjoy Life

We are hedged in (pressed) on every side [troubled and oppressed in every way], but not cramped or crushed; we suffer embarrassments and are perplexed and unable to find a way out, but not driven to despair; we are pursued (persecuted and hard driven), but not deserted [to stand alone]; we are struck down to the ground, but never struck out and destroyed; always carrying about in the body the liability and exposure to the same putting to death that the Lord Jesus suffered....

2 Corinthians 4:8-10

A great lie and deception from Satan is that we cannot enjoy our lives in the midst of unpleasant circumstances. A study of the life of Jesus proves otherwise, as does the life of Paul, and many others. Actually, they knew that joy was a spiritual force that would help them overcome their problems.

In John 16 Jesus warned His disciples about many of the hardships and persecutions that they would face in this life, concluding in verse 33: **I have told you these things, so that in Me you may have [perfect] peace and confidence. In the world you have tribulation and trials and distress and frustration; but be of good cheer [take courage; be confident, certain, undaunted]! For I have overcome the world. [I have deprived it of power to harm you and have conquered it for you.]**

Jesus was saying to His followers, "When you have problems—and you will have them in this world—*cheer up!*"

If you don't really understand His heart here, it could almost sound as if Jesus is not being very compassionate. But actually, He is sharing a "spiritual secret":

... **The joy of the Lord is your strength** (Neh. 8:10 KJV).

Joy as a Weapon

[We pray] that you may be invigorated and strengthened with all power according to the

might of His glory, [to exercise] every kind of endurance and patience (perseverance and forbearance) with joy.

                                              Colossians 1:11

Paul prayed for the Colossians that they would endure with joy. Why with joy? Because joy enables us to enjoy the journey.

If you and I can never enjoy our lives until the time comes when we have no adverse circumstances, we will live in sadness and never know the joy Jesus intended for us. I also believe that joy, and the expression of it, is a weapon of spiritual warfare, as well as a fruit of the Holy Spirit.

Joy as a Fruit of the Spirit

And you [set yourselves to] become imitators of us and [through us] of the Lord Himself, for you welcomed our message in [spite of] much persecution, with joy [inspired] by the Holy Spirit.

                                        1 Thessalonians 1:6

The believers in Thessalonica were being persecuted for their faith, and yet Paul wrote that they endured the persecution with joy. According to Galatians 5:22, joy is a fruit of the Spirit—not sadness or depression, not frowning or scowling.

If we will remain filled with the Holy Spirit, He will inspire or energize us to be joyful, in spite of our outward circumstances.

I believe the lack of joy is why many times we give up when we should endure. I also believe that the presence of joy gives us the endurance to outlast the devil, overcome our negative circumstances and have the abundant life Jesus died to give us.

Guard Your Mind, Watch Your Mouth!

This Book of the Law shall not depart out of your mouth, but you shall meditate on it day and night, that you may observe and do according to all that is written in it. For then you shall make your way prosperous, and then you shall deal wisely and have good success.

Joshua 1:8

Joshua had plenty of enemies to confront on his journey. As a matter of fact, it seemed there was a never-ending parade of them. But please notice that Joshua was instructed by the Lord to keep the *Word* in his mouth and in his mind, not the *problem*.

Like Joshua, if you and I are to make our way prosperous and have good success in this life, we will definitely need to put our thoughts and words on something other than the problem that faces us. We need to stop thinking about the problem, talking about the problem and, sometimes, we even need to stop praying about the problem. If we have prayed, God has heard.

I am not saying there is not a time for persistent prayer, but we don't want to be fellowshipping with our problem in prayer, rather than God Himself.

In Mark 11:23 Jesus instructed us to *speak to* the mountain. He did not say, *"Talk about* the mountain." If there is a purpose in talking about it, then do so. Otherwise, it is best to give it to God in prayer and then keep quiet about it. Words stir up emotions that often cause us to become upset and remain focused on the circumstance.

It is valuable to go out and do something enjoyable while you are waiting for God to solve your problem. You may not feel like it, but do it anyway.

It will help you!

Get your mind—and your mouth—off the problem!

Have and Enjoy Life—Now!

We always think we will enjoy life when our breakthrough comes. But what about enjoying the trip—the time of waiting—the journey?

I certainly do not mean to sound negative, but when the breakthrough you and I have been waiting for finally comes, it won't be long until we will be faced with another challenge. If we wait to enjoy life until we have no problems, we may never have much enjoyment.

Let God take care of your problems; cast your care upon Him and do what He has instructed you to do. It almost sounds too good to be true, but you can actually *enjoy* life while God handles all your problems!

The Value of Laughter

He [God] will rescue you in six troubles; in seven nothing that is evil [for you] will touch you.

In famine He will redeem you from death, and in war from the power of the sword.

You shall be hidden from the scourge of the tongue, neither shall you be afraid of destruction when it comes.

At destruction and famine you shall laugh, neither shall you be afraid of the living creatures of the earth.

Job 5:19-22 (emphasis added)

There are some really awesome Scriptures in the Bible about the value of laughter, which is an expression of joy. Job 5:19-22 is one of my favorite passages on this subject. In verse 22 we are told that we will *laugh* at destruction and famine, and in Psalm 2:2-4, we see that this is how God speaks of how He handles His enemies.

Find the Right Opportunities to Laugh

I have changed a lot in this area recently. A few years ago I probably passed up many opportunities to laugh. I was too busy being serious and intense. Now, when opportunity comes my way, I enter in and get the most out of it. I know I need to laugh—and so do you.

Laughter and a happy heart must be cultivated. Jesus talked about joy and fullness of joy. I want all I can have of both, but it takes a conscious effort to keep our hearts merry. Satan is always willing to steal or block our joy, and he will do so if we allow it.

Laughter and smiling are outward evidences of inward

joy. The world cannot see our heart; they need to see the expression of what's in our heart. Our general attitude should be pleasant, abundant with smiles, and if the situation is right, we should laugh whenever possible.

We should never laugh at someone else's expense, make fun of their flaws or be rude. I want to encourage you to make a decision to laugh more but remember to be sensitive to the place, timing and people around you.

Being in God's presence brings us joy, and the Bible teaches us that the climate of heaven is joyful, which means there is laughter going on there too!

Psalm 16:11 says, **You will show me the path of life; in Your presence is fullness of joy, at Your right hand there are pleasures forevermore.**

I have experienced laughter many times while spending time with God. His presence always makes me happy.

Stay Strong by Refusing to Lose Your Joy!

You [Lord] meet and spare him who joyfully works righteousness (uprightness and justice), [earnestly] remembering You in Your ways....

Isaiah 64:5

In the *New King James Version* of this verse, the prophet

says, **You** [Lord] **meet him who rejoices and does righteousness....**

Since you and I are the righteousness of God in Christ (2 Cor. 5:21), when we rejoice, God will meet us at the point of our need and see us through to the finish line. A rejoicing heart is not a heavy heart; it is one full of singing. As He did with Paul and Silas in the Philippian jail, God will give us a song in our "midnight hour" (Acts 16:25).

In Isaiah 61:3 KJV the prophet said that the Lord gives a garment of praise for the spirit of heaviness, and in Romans 4:18-20, we read what Abraham did during the time of his waiting for the Lord to fulfill His promises to him:

[For Abraham, human reason for] hope being gone, hoped in faith that he should become the father of many nations, as he had been promised, So [numberless] shall your descendants be.

He did not weaken in faith when he considered the [utter] impotence of his own body, which was as good as dead because he was about a hundred years old, or [when he considered] the barrenness of Sarah's [deadened] womb.

No unbelief or distrust made him waver (doubtingly question) concerning the promise of God, but *he grew strong and was empowered by faith as he gave praise and glory to God.*

Abraham did not permit his heart to become heavy; instead, he kept up his faith and his spirit by giving praise and glory to God.

I believe Abraham kept a merry heart, and therefore, his faith was strengthened to carry him through to the end.

Wells of Joy

Now on the final and most important day of the Feast, Jesus stood, and He cried in a loud voice, If any man is thirsty, let him come to Me and drink!

He who believes in Me [who cleaves to and trusts in and relies on Me] as the Scripture has said, From his innermost being shall flow [continuously] springs and rivers of living water.

But He was speaking here of the Spirit, Whom those who believed (trusted, had faith) in Him were afterward to receive. For the [Holy] Spirit had not yet been given, because Jesus was not yet glorified (raised to honor).

John 7:37-39

When we have the Holy Spirit living in us, we have righteousness, peace and joy living in us (Rom. 14:17 KJV). Our inner man is like a well of good things (Matt. 12:35).

One of those good things is joy. But Satan will try to stop up our well.

Actually, stopping up the wells of one's enemies was a warfare strategy used in days past, as we see in 2 Kings 3:19: **You shall smite every fenced city and every choice city, and shall fell every good tree and stop all wells of water and mar every good piece of land with stones.**

The stones of worry, self-pity, depression—all of these things—are Satan's strategy to stop up your well. When your soul is full of these stones, it hinders the flow of God's Spirit within you. God wants to unstop your well! He desires that the river of life in you flow freely.

Let joy flow! Let peace flow!

Our own efforts always bring misery and frustration, but God's promise will bring joy and laughter.

Laughter will help unstop the well of living water that the Holy Spirit brings to our soul!

Maybe you have not laughed—I mean really laughed—in a very long time. You will find that you feel better all over after a hearty laugh.

Sometimes I feel as if my pipes have been cleaned out, so to speak, after a good laugh. If I am tired and weary from dealing with life's issues, I often feel like a dusty closet inside—stale and in need of refreshing. When God provides me with opportunity to have a really good laugh, it seems to "air me out"—to refresh me and lift the load off my tired mind.

The Proper Balance

There should be a balance between soberness and laughter. The Bible teaches both. 1Peter 5:8 says to be **sober of mind,** but it does not say to be sober-faced. Matthew 5:14 states that we are **the light of the world.** You might say that a smile is like the switch that turns the lamp on. There is not much chance of laughter if we do not start with a smile.

If we have a frown on our face, with the corners of our mouth turned down, it can drag us down emotionally.

When I frown, I can literally feel a heaviness. (Go ahead and try it; I think you will feel the same thing.) But when I smile, I sense a lifting of my entire countenance.

I can be all by myself and smile. I don't even need anything in particular to smile about. It just makes me feel happier to smile occasionally, even when I am alone. I might add that I have, by nature, always been a very serious-minded, sober-faced individual, and if I can learn to smile, anyone who is really willing can do the same.

It takes a lot more facial muscles to frown than it does to smile. Some of us probably have weak muscles from lack of use, but they will build up in a short period of time.

Go ahead and try it. Act like a little child. Frown and see how you feel—then smile and see how you feel.

There are two good reasons to learn to smile. First, it helps you look and feel better. Second, it helps those around you.

One of the ways we can show the world the joy that comes from abiding in Jesus is by looking happy. When the peace and joy of the Lord are a regular part of our countenance, it speaks a silent message to those with whom we intermingle.

Proverbs 17:22 says, **A happy heart is good medicine and a cheerful mind works healing, but a broken spirit dries up the bones.** Pray and ask God to help you remember to smile often. Take your medicine—laugh more!

10

Diversity and Creativity

And they [the apostles] went out and preached everywhere, while the Lord kept working with them and confirming the message by the attesting signs and miracles that closely accompanied [it]....

Mark 16:20

I hope that by the time you have reached this point in the book you are already starting to enjoy life more. I believe whatever we study about in God's Word, we can believe God for signs and wonders in that area.

According to Mark, the apostles went everywhere preaching the Word, and God confirmed the Word with "signs and miracles" Acts 5:12 says that **by the hands of the apostles ... numerous and startling signs and wonders were being performed among the people.**

I used to think that those signs and wonders would only be miraculous physical healings until God began showing me that I also needed to expect miraculous breakthroughs and healing in whatever area I was teaching about in His Word. So I am certainly believing that everyone who reads this book will enter into a new level of joy and enjoyment.

There are many reasons why people do not enjoy their lives, and no matter how lengthy this book might be, I could never cover all of those reasons. But I do want to emphasize the importance of diversity and creativity in maintaining the "spice in life," which helps keep joy flowing.

Because too much of the same things can be a thief of joy.

God Likes Variety!

Behold, I am doing a new thing! Now it springs forth; do you not perceive and know it and will you not give heed to it?....

Isaiah 43:19

Do you ever get just plain bored—just really tired of doing the same old thing all the time? You want to do something different but you either don't know what to do, or you are afraid to do the new thing you are thinking about doing. You may have these feelings because we were all created for variety.

I believe God has put creativity in all of us. He is certainly creative and believes in variety. Think of all the varieties of birds, flowers, trees, grass, etc. that He has created. People come in a never-ending variety of sizes, shapes and colors, with different personalities.

All of our fingerprints are different. There is not another human being in the world with your fingerprints. The various nations in our world and all of the different customs and manner of dress are awesome because they reveal God's creativity and love of variety.

Foods and their preparation vary greatly from nation to nation. Italian food is quite different from Chinese or Mexican food. In America, we find the food in the South to be different from that in the North.

God likes variety!

Diversity and Imagination

And out of the ground the Lord God formed every [wild] beast and living creature of the field and every bird of the air and brought them to Adam to see what he would call them; and whatever Adam called every living creature, that was its name.

And Adam gave names to all the livestock and to the birds of the air and to every [wild] beast of the field....

Genesis 2:19-20

I cannot imagine what kind of a job it must have been for Adam to name all the birds and animals. He certainly had to be creative to do it.

I could go on and on about how diverse and imaginative God was in Creation, but I am sure if you think about it a little, you will agree that our God is an awesome God.

Simply take a walk and look around you. If it will help you, put this book down and take a walk now. Download or rent a few nature videos. Find out what is in the ocean, or how bees and flowers work together. Then realize that the same Holy Spirit present at Creation is living inside of you if you have truly accepted Jesus Christ as your Lord and Savior (Acts 2:38).

There is a lot of creativity inside each of us that we need to tap into without fear.

I think we often get into ruts. We do the same thing all the time even though we are bored with it because we are afraid to step out and do something different. *We would rather be safe and bored than excited and living on the edge.* There is a certain amount of comfort in sameness. We may not like it, but we are familiar with it.

Some people stay in jobs or professions all their lives because what they are doing is safe. They may hate their job and feel completely unfulfilled, but the thought of doing anything else is frightening and holds them back. Or maybe they do think and dream about a change, but their dreams will never manifest because they are afraid of failure, so they will not do their part to see their dreams come to pass.

I do not advocate jumping out in the middle of every "whim" that comes along, but there is a definite time to step out of the ordinary, out of your comfort zone, and into new things.

God has created you and me to need and crave diversity and variety. We are created to require freshness and newness in our lives. There is nothing wrong with us if we feel sometimes that we just need a change. On the other hand, if we can never be satisfied for very long no matter what we are doing, then we have the reverse problem.

The Word of God instructs us to be content and satisfied (Heb. 13:5; 1 Tim. 6:6). Once again we find that *balance* is the key.

Be Well Balanced

Be well balanced (temperate, sober of mind), be vigilant and cautious at all times; for that enemy of yours, the devil, roams around like a lion roaring [in fierce hunger], seeking someone to seize upon and devour.

1 Peter 5:8

People can definitely get out of balance by doing too much of one thing or another, and when that happens, a door is opened for the devil, as we see in this verse.

Even unbalanced eating habits can open a door for poor health. The Word of God instructs us to do all things in moderation (1 Cor. 9:25). We have heard all of our lives from childhood that we need a balanced diet: plenty of good protein, a variety of fruits, vegetables, seeds, nuts and grains, and lots of water.

Eventually there will be a price to pay if we don't obey natural laws. Today, we can take vitamins and other food supplements to help compensate for some of the missing nutrients in our diet, but balance is vital.

I remember when my youngest son disliked vegetables. He would eat canned green beans if we made him, but that was it. I would tell him all the time, "Daniel, you need to eat vegetables. You're missing a whole food group that has things in it you need. God wouldn't have put them here if we didn't need them."

It is amazing how many people do not like and will not drink water, which is very important for good, lasting health. Often such likes and dislikes are evidence of a certain mindset, and until they change their minds, the situation will not improve.

One of my good friends grew up in a family situation in which the dinner table was where the family met to argue.

Thus, she grew to hate family mealtimes. She ate a lot of junk food in her late teens and young adult years. She did so partially because she did not want to plan proper meals.

She did not enjoy thinking about meal preparation, so when she did get hungry, she grabbed whatever was quick. As she grew older, she began to realize that she probably needed to do something to change her eating habits, but she still felt that she just could not be bothered with planning ahead where food was concerned.

Then she had a time of sickness in her life, and at one point, it was severe enough to frighten her. That's when she *decided* she had to do something about her diet. It was truly amazing how quickly she changed once she had made a quality decision.

This same principle works in anything. People who think they cannot exercise find they can if they decide to do it and stick with their decision. People who have had a lifelong problem with certain issues often find, through the teaching of God's Word, that much of their problem is tied to wrong thinking.

We *can* live balanced lives. Without balance, things get lopsided—there is too much of one thing and not enough of another. Physical sickness, relationship problems and certainly loss of joy can all be the result of unbalanced living.

Human nature without the Holy Spirit tends to get into

extremes, and left unrestrained, it will lead to major trouble. We need the fruit of self-discipline in our lives (Gal. 5:22-23) so we can be led by the Spirit and not our extreme cravings and desires.

Imbalance and Boredom Cause Problems

Perhaps you are not resting enough or laughing enough, or maybe you are working too hard. Too much stress, frequent emotional upset and a lack of variety in life can all have adverse effects on your health.

God dealt with me about having balance in my eating habits, but the principle should be applied in every area of life. Once you learn the principle of balance, moderation, variety and diversity, you can apply it to relationships, spending, eating, work habits, dress standards, entertainment and many other things.

When we come home from our ministry trips, I love to just be at home. I prefer to eat at home when possible, and I like to watch good, clean family movies at home when they are available. I like to sit and relax with a cup of tea or coffee and look out the windows. I just like to *be* there.

But I have noticed that after about three days, I start getting bored with what I was loving three days before. There is nothing wrong with me. It is just my God-given nature, letting me know that it is time for something different.

I believe God builds these warning signs into us, and if we will pay attention to them, it will keep us out of serious trouble. Our emotional makeup needs change. Denying ourselves necessary variety because of fear or insecurity—or for any other reason—is dangerous. If we do so, we are headed for a great loss of joy.

The fine art of balance is a delicate thing, and each of us must listen to the Holy Spirit and to our own heart. We each have individual needs, and I find it fascinating how one person really needs something that another doesn't need at all.

I have had the same hairstyle—or one similar to it-- for years and years and probably will never change it. But I don't like to wear the same pajamas more than two nights, so I have several pair, and I switch them around so I don't get bored with my nightwear.

My daughter, Laura, on the other hand, changes her hairstyle about twice a year. She tries all kinds of new things—many of which she doesn't like—but she likes change in her hair. Yet, it does not matter at all to her what she sleeps in.

For this reason, we cannot look to other people's lifestyles and choices to tell us what to do. One individual may be totally satisfied eating the same thing for breakfast every day of his life, while another one may want hot cereal one morning and eggs the next, then cold cereal with bananas, then fruit, then bagels with cream cheese.

Remember that variety means just that, and you are free to have variety within your variety. In other words, you are free to be *you;* you don't have to follow someone else's plan.

Don't Get Stale and Moldy!

This bread of ours we took hot for our provision from our houses on the day we departed to come to you. But now look, it is dry and moldy.

Joshua 9:12 NKJV

If I have a loaf of bread on the table at dinner, and after dinner, we sit, talk a while and drink coffee, I can reach out and touch the bread that is not covered up and tell if it is starting to get a little dry around the edges. It may not be stale yet, but if I don't wrap it up and take proper care of it, it will soon become hard, brittle and tasteless.

The same principle applies to our lives. If we are not careful, the enemy will deceive us into allowing our lives to become dry and stale.

We must learn to resist the devil at his onset!

Years ago, our daughter Sandra helped us as our full-time housekeeper. She spent a lot of time cleaning and doing laundry. Anyone who cleans house day after day can get tired of it. It may be one of the hardest jobs to stay excited about, because you clean it and someone else messes it up, and you clean it again, and it gets messed up all over again. This is especially true when small children or teenagers are present.

I noticed once that Sandra was doing jobs on Monday that she normally did later in the week, so I asked her, "What are you doing?"

"I've got to mix this schedule up some way," she answered, "and get a little bit of freshness into it."

You see, sometimes it helps if you just change your laundry day, or, for diversion, watch a movie or listen to music while you iron. Try going to the grocery store on a different day, or even better, go to a different store. These simple change-ups can add enough variety to keep things from getting too stale.

My administrative assistant was a perfectionist who has now been liberated from compulsive behavior. In the past, she would never have left her house without the bed being made. She began to see the need for some diversity in her life so she said to me one day, "You are going to laugh when I tell you this."

She went on to say that just for some diversion, she had purposely left her house that morning with the bed unmade. She said she thoroughly enjoyed walking out and looking back at it messed up. This was a sign of freedom and liberty for her.

"I will only do it for this week," she said, "but it sure has felt good just to get out of the mold."

When she said that, it occurred to me that *if we stay in the same mold too long, we become moldy!*

Our youngest son, who was eleven at the time and not fond of making his bed or cleaning his room, overheard my assistant's story. The next day he said to me, "Well, I'm going to have a little variety today. I'm not going to make my bed."

Of course, he was trying to be funny; he probably thought he had "bed-making burnout," but I wanted him to keep making his bed and burn on.

Some people say, "I have to have a routine," or "I'm just a creature of habit." Routine is good, and some habits are also good, as long as they don't lead to staleness and moldiness.

You are free to be as routine-driven or habit-oriented as you like, as long as you have joy with it. The important thing is that you make an effort to see how much you can *enjoy* your life!

Add Variety in Simple Ways

. . . if only I may finish my course with joy. . . .

Acts 20:24

Adding variety to your life does not have to be expensive or complicated. If you want to do something different in the evening, take the family for an outing. Most young children love to take a ride in the car. Even thirty minutes can be just what all of you need.

Go out and get a cup of coffee. Yes, you could make it at home, but it might not be as much fun. Go get an ice cream cone or a soda. Go for a walk, or sit at the park and watch the children play. During holidays take a ride around the neighborhood and look at the Christmas lights on houses.

If you have a big project in front of you that is going to be an all-day task, take a few short breaks. Walk outside for a few minutes if the weather is nice and drink a glass of iced tea. If you see your neighbors out, talk with them for a while. Go sit on the couch and watch a short program on TV that you enjoy.

You must never lose sight of your goal, but those short breaks can make all the difference in how you feel about the project. It can help you "finish your course with joy."

Whatever you do, if you are obeying Scripture and doing it unto the Lord, you should not only start the course with joy, but also finish it the same way.

11

Joy in God's Waiting Room

A man's mind plans his way, but the Lord directs his steps and makes them sure.

Proverbs 16:9

We think and plan in temporal terms, and God thinks and plans in eternal terms. What this means is that we are very interested in right now, and God is much more interested in eternity. We want what "feels good" right now, and what produces immediate results, but God is willing to invest time. God is an investor; He will invest a lot of time in us because He has an eternal purpose planned for our lives.

God sees and understands what we don't see and understand. He asks us to trust Him, not to live based on our own understanding, which is frustrating when things don't always go according to our plan.

Without abundant trust in God, we will never experience

joy and enjoyment. We have ideas about how and when things should happen. Not only does God have a predetermined plan for our lives, but He has the perfect timing for each phase. Psalm 31:15 assures us that our times are in His hands. Fighting and resisting the timing of God is equivalent to fighting His will.

Many times we fail to realize that being out of God's timing is the same as being out of His will. We may know *what* God wants us to do, but not *when* He wants us to do it.

Give God Time!

After these things, the word of the Lord came to Abram in a vision, saying, Fear not, Abram, I am your Shield, your abundant compensation, and your reward shall be exceedingly great.

And Abram said, Lord God, what can You give me, since I am going on [from this world] childless and he who shall be the owner and heir of my house is this [steward] Eliezer of Damascus?

And Abram continued, Look, You have given me no child; and [a servant] born in my house is my heir.

And behold, the word of the Lord came to him, saying, This man shall not be your heir, but he who shall come from your own body shall be your heir.

> **And He brought him outside [his tent into the
> starlight] and said, Look now toward the heavens
> and count the stars—if you are able to number them.
> Then He said to him, So shall your descendants be.**
> **Genesis 15:1-5**

Abraham had a very definite word from God about his future. He knew what God had promised, but had no word regarding when it would take place.

The same is often true for us. While we are waiting for our promise or dream to come together—waiting for the breakthrough—it is not always easy to enjoy the time spent in the waiting room.

Once God speaks to us or shows us something, we are filled up with it. It is as though we are "pregnant" with what God has said. He has planted a seed in us, and we must enter a time of preparation. This time prepares us to handle the thing that God has promised to give us or do for us.

It is very much like the birth of a child. First, the seed is planted in the womb, then come nine months of waiting, and finally, a baby is born. During those nine months, there is a great deal that is happening. The woman's body is changing to prepare her to be able to give birth. The seed is growing into maturity. The parents are preparing things for the baby's arrival. They are accumulating the necessary equipment to properly care for a child.

Just as there is a lot of activity inside the mother's body that we cannot see, so there is a lot of activity in the spiritual world concerning God's promises to us. Just because we cannot see or feel anything happening does not mean that nothing is taking place. God does some of His best work in secret, and He delights in surprising His children.

Ishmael Is Not Isaac

Now Sarai, Abram's wife, had borne him no children. She had an Egyptian maid whose name was Hagar.

And Sarai said to Abram, See here, the Lord has restrained me from bearing [children]. I am asking you to have intercourse with my maid; it may be that I can obtain children by her. And Abram listened to and heeded what Sarai said.

Genesis 16:1-2

Abraham and Sarah got tired of waiting. They were weary and began to wonder if maybe there was something they could do to help things move along faster. In Genesis 16:1-2, we see that Sarah (then called Sarai), Abram's wife, had an idea to give her handmaiden to her husband that he might have intercourse with her. She felt perhaps this would be God's way of giving them the promised child. It seemed to her that God was not doing anything, so she would do something.

Does that sound familiar? During the waiting times, do you ever get a bright idea and try to help the Holy Spirit?

Abraham listened to Sarah, did what she asked, and the result was the birth of a child called Ishmael. But Ishmael was not the child of promise.

Ishmael was fourteen years old when Isaac, the child of promise, was finally born. It probably took longer than originally planned, because once we give birth to the "Ishmaels" in our lives, we have to deal with the repercussions. I always say that once we have Ishmael, we have to change his diapers and take care of him.

We would like to do our own thing and have God make it work out, but He let me know years ago that what we give birth to in the strength of our own flesh, He is not obligated to care for or pay for.

Ishmael never brings us joy. We may love him, because we certainly love the fruit of our labors. What we struggle and labor to bring forth usually means a lot to us, but that does not mean it has the inherent ability to bring enjoyment to our lives.

There are many frustrated people with no joy who have established and oversee major works. God did not say we could not build, but the psalmist did say, **Except the Lord builds the house, they labor in vain who build it . . .** (Ps. 127:1).

It is terribly frustrating to labor and build and have all the visible signs of success, yet have no ability to enjoy it. We can build, but if our labor is not in God's plan for us, it can be in vain (useless).

Many people spend their lives climbing the ladder of success and find when they reach the top that their ladder is leaning against the wrong building. I don't want to do that with my life, and I'm sure you don't want to do that with yours either.

It is vitally important to realize that whatever God calls us to do, He provides enjoyment for us to do it. God has not drawn you and me into relationship with Himself in order to make us miserable. Instead, He brings us righteousness, peace and joy (Rom. 14:17).

Many people have no joy from their labors, but this should not be so for the Spirit-led children of God. Enjoying our labor is a gift from God (Eccl. 5:19). Enjoyment itself is a gift from God, and a blessed one I might add. I know what it's like to work without enjoyment, and I don't ever want to live like that again.

Ishmael Cannot Be Heir with Isaac

The Lord visited Sarah as He had said, and the Lord did for her as He had promised.

> For Sarah became pregnant and bore Abraham a son in his old age, at the set time God had told him.
>
> Abraham named his son whom Sarah bore to him Isaac [laughter].
>
> **Genesis 21:1-3**

Isaac was finally born, and he and Ishmael were raised together for three years, but not without some challenges.

In Genesis 21:10, Sarah told Abraham that Ishmael had to go, and God confirmed her words in verse 12 saying, . . . **Do not let it seem grievous and evil to you because of the youth and your bondwoman; in all that Sarah has said to you, do what she asks, for in Isaac shall your posterity be called.**

Ishmael could not be heir with Isaac. The work of the flesh could not share in the work of the Lord.

There always comes a time when the works of our own flesh must experience death or total separation. God wants us to be inheritors, not laborers. We are heirs of God and joint-heirs with Jesus Christ (Rom. 8:17 NKJV). An heir receives what another has worked for. He doesn't work himself to obtain what is already his, by inheritance. And if he tries to, he will definitely lose his joy.

Genesis 16:12 KJV says that Ishmael **will be a wild man; his hand will be against every man, and every man's hand**

against him.... while Isaac's name means "laughter." This really says it all.

When we do our own thing in our own timing and refuse to wait on God, we are going to get war. When we wait for God's promise, it will always bring us joy. The waiting is difficult, but the joy of receiving the prize is worth the wait. How to enjoy the waiting is the key.

God's Timing Is Not for Us to Know

He [Jesus] said to them [the disciples], It is not for you to become acquainted with and know what time brings [the things and events of time and their definite periods] or fixed years and seasons (their critical niche in time), which the Father has appointed (fixed and reserved) by His own choice and authority and personal power.

Acts 1:7

Often we experience a lot of disappointment, which hinders joy and enjoyment, due to deciding for ourselves that something has to be done a certain way, or by a certain time. When we want something very strongly, we can easily convince ourselves that it is God's will for us to have it when we want it, the way we want it.

I always believe and pray for things. I am goal-oriented and always need something to look forward to. Many years ago, I struggled with frustration when things didn't happen the way I thought they should. I attempted to use my faith to get what I wanted. When it did not arrive on time, I felt my faith was weak, or that the enemy was blocking my blessing.

Now, after many years of experience walking closely with God, I know that I can and should use my faith, but God has an appointed time.

"In due time" (1 Pet. 5:6), "at the appointed time" (Gen. 18:14), at "the proper time" (Gal. 4:4)—these are things the Bible says about God's timing. Jesus Himself made it clear that it is not for us to know what these times are.

Remaining expectant every day, trusting God to make His plans come to pass no matter how long it takes, is one of the things that will keep you and me flowing in joy.

When a pregnant woman is waiting to deliver her child, people say that she is "expecting." I am sure most of us are expecting.

I know I am expecting.

There are things God has spoken to me—things He has placed in my heart—that I have not experienced yet. Some of them have been there as long as fifteen or sixteen years. Other things He put in my heart around the same time have already come to pass.

I used to be confused by this. Now, I am no longer confused, I am expecting. My time can come at any moment, any day—maybe even today. And so can yours.

Suddenly!

We can expect "a season of suddenlies" in our lives. We can get up in the morning with a major problem and go to bed without it.

God moves suddenly.

Actually, He is working behind the scenes all the time, but just as the birth of a baby comes suddenly, so God manifests what He has been doing for us suddenly!

In Acts 1:4, after His resurrection, Jesus instructed His disciples and other followers...**not to leave Jerusalem but to wait for what the Father had promised, of which [He said] you have heard Me speak.** They were instructed to wait.

It is hard on us when God's instruction to us is to wait. There have been times when I have said to the Lord, "What do You want me to do?" And all He said was, "Wait." He did not tell me how long—just to wait.

We must be willing to wait indefinitely.

In Acts 1:13, we read what the disciples did after Jesus gave them the instructions to wait and then left them behind as He ascended to the Father in heaven: **And when** they had entered [the city], they mounted [the stairs] to the upper room, where they were [*indefinitely*] staying. . . . When they went into the upper room, they did not place a time limit on how long they would wait. They had heard from Jesus, and they intended to obey.

Then in Acts 2:1-2, we are told what happened as they waited: **And when the day of Pentecost had fully come, they were all assembled together in one place, when *suddenly* there came a sound from heaven like the rushing of a violent tempest blast, and it filled the whole house in which they were sitting.**

As they waited—*suddenly*—what they were waiting for arrived.

Just think of it: one minute they were waiting, and the next minute they had what they had been anticipating. That makes life exciting!

We can expect and be full of hope.

A pregnant woman, when her time comes near, goes to bed each evening thinking, "This could be the night." She awakens each day thinking, "Maybe today I will have the baby." She continues in that frame of mind until the blessed event takes place.

We should have that same attitude, and as we do, we will enjoy the trip. We can enjoy the waiting room, but only with the proper attitude.

The Silent Years

Jesus spent thirty years in preparation for a three-year ministry.

Most of us might be willing to prepare three weeks for a thirty-year ministry, and even at that, we would rather it not take so long. We are so accustomed to our "instant, everything now" society that we bring these impatient expectations into our relationship with God. It keeps us in a state of turmoil until we see that God is not going to promote us before we are thoroughly prepared.

In His humanity, Jesus went through some things that equipped Him to do what God had called Him to do, as we read in Hebrews 5:8-9: **Although He [Jesus] was a Son, He learned [active, special] obedience through what He suffered and, [His completed experience] making Him perfectly [equipped], He became the Author and Source of eternal salvation to all those who give heed and obey Him.**

Jesus had what I call "silent years," and so did many other Bible heroes who were mightily used by God.

The birth of Jesus is recorded in Luke chapter 2. He was circumcised when He was eight days old according to the Law, and shortly after, He was dedicated in the temple, but we hear nothing else about Him in the Scriptures until

He was twelve years old. Then, we find Him in the temple sitting among the teachers and asking questions (Luke 2:41-51).

The only thing I can find in the Word of God regarding those "silent years" is that He...**grew and became strong in spirit, filled with wisdom; and the grace (favor and spiritual blessing) of God was upon Him** (Luke 2:40).

Between the ages of twelve and thirty, Jesus had more "silent years"—eighteen years when nobody heard anything about Him. He had to be doing something. What? After His parents found Him in the temple when He was supposed to have gone home with them, they took Him back with them: **And He went down with them and came to Nazareth and was [habitually] obedient to them; and his mother kept and closely and persistently guarded all these things in her heart. And Jesus increased in wisdom (in broad and full understanding) and in stature and years, and in favor with God and man** (Luke 2:51-52). This is another way of saying, "He grew."

Just as Jesus grew during this quiet time, so you and I must grow in many things; the silent years help to provide that growth.

During these years we gain strength as we learn and go through various things. It is a principle of life that everything grows. Faith grows, wisdom grows, along with knowledge, comprehension and understanding.

Discernment develops as well as sensitivity to people and to God. The Word of God teaches us, but so do life's experiences, as we see in Proverbs 5:1: **My son, be attentive to my Wisdom [godly Wisdom learned by actual and costly experience], and incline your ear to my understanding [of what is becoming and prudent for you].**

I remember the "silent years" in my life—years when I knew God had call me into ministry—but nothing was happening. Those were years when I was believing but not seeing.

We all have times when we feel that nothing is happening and it seems that no one, not even God, really even cares. We can't seem to hear from God. We can't "feel" God. We wonder if we are a little "flaky," or maybe we never heard from God after all.

Those are times when it seems as if God has placed us neatly on a shelf, and we wonder if He will ever use us, or if we will ever experience our breakthrough.

These are the times when we need to remember by faith that God has an appointed time, and His timing is perfect!

Hurrying Steals Joy

God has spent a lot of time teaching me that hurrying steals joy. Because He is not in a hurry, or, we might say, He does not have a "hurry up" spirit about Him, neither should we. After all, we are created in His image.

Can you imagine Jesus behaving the way we do? I doubt that He got up in the morning and began telling the disciples to hurry up and get ready so they could get on over to Jerusalem and hold a conference.

Not only does God have a timing concerning when we will experience the desires and goals we are waiting for, but I also believe there is a timing that we are to live in. Perhaps I should say, a speed at which we are to live. It should show up in our pace in life. How we walk, talk and eat reveals something about our attitude toward waiting.

There is a pace that is comfortable to walk at, but the "hurry up" spirit that prevails in the earth today makes us want to rush and do things that don't even require rushing. Some people talk so fast you can hardly take in and digest what they are saying. Others become irritated if you don't understand them immediately, and asking them to repeat or explain something usually makes them upset.

Many people don't really eat, they devour their food. Sometimes people who eat too fast have problems with overeating. I believe there is an emotional satisfaction that we obtain from eating. Not only do our bodies need the nourishment, but we are to enjoy our meals. If we take time to enjoy them thoroughly, we may find that we are more satisfied and require less food.

People are just generally in a hurry. So often today when we ask others how they are, they respond with, "Busy." That automatically makes me feel rushed. I get the impression that they wish I hadn't stopped them and they just wanted to be left alone. Most people are definitely living life in the fast lane, but it is not the lane in which we would find Jesus if He were living in the flesh on the earth today.

Make a decision not to live your life in a hurry. You won't enjoy it if you rush through it. Everything will go by in a blur.

Often people complain about how busy they are—how tired they are—but they don't do anything about it.

Make a decision! Taste life! Savor the flavor of each day. Take some time each evening to ponder the day's events, especially the little special things that happened.

Meditate on the things that brought you joy, and you can have the pleasure of enjoying them all over again. If you are going to have to hurry all the time in order to do what you are doing, make a decision to do less.

Is getting out of your house in the morning on time a nightmare of rushing and frustration? Make a decision to do less, or get up earlier. Declare war on the spirit of "hurry up"!

Too often we are either overcommitted or undercommitted. What we really need is balanced commitments. God is not impressed with our excessive activity, even when it is done in His name. Remember that peace leads to joy. If Satan can steal our peace, then he will also get our joy.

12

Freedom in Relationships

For you, brethren, were [indeed] called to freedom....
Galatians 5:13

When it comes to enjoying life, we are all at different places on our journey. Some of us enjoy life thoroughly, and others not at all. Some enjoy it a little, and some have never even realized that they should enjoy life thoroughly.

Think about what I said earlier. Jesus said He came that we might have and enjoy life, and that we might have it in abundance—to the full until it overflows (John 10:10). We are commanded to enjoy our lives, at least that is the way I have decided to look at it.

To enjoy life, we must have liberty, and we must allow others to have liberty.

Some of the hardest work we can take on is the job of trying to control those around us.

I spent a lot of years trying to control my husband, my children and my friends. I was not doing it because I was mean. As a child, I had been abused and controlled myself, and I think somewhere along the way, I decided it was either control or be controlled. I was afraid to let others lead because I felt that if I did, I would never get anything I wanted.

My experience had been that anyone who had any authority in my life had hurt me, and I was not going to let that happen again. I did not really even understand that I was a controller—that I had become the very thing I hated.

I did understand that I was not happy. I had no peace and joy, and I surely was not enjoying my life. I knew I had a problem, but I did not know what it was or how to fix it.

I have been sharing chapter by chapter the things that God has shown me during my own recovery, and this chapter is no exception. This is something I have learned that has immensely helped me to enjoy my life and all the people in it.

Not only did I have a problem with attempting to control others, but in certain ways, I allowed people to control me. I was overly concerned about what they thought. I tried to live up to their expectations and silent demands.

This was the case especially among groups of people with whom I desired to be in relationship. I wanted to be a part, but was still on the outside looking in. It seems to me now as I look back, that I tried to control those who loved me, and lived in the fear of rejection of the people whose love I desperately wanted. As a result, I allowed them to steal my liberty.

God did not create us for any kind of control except

self-control. We are to willingly give Him the reins to our lives, not try to keep them, nor give them to people who want to use us for their own benefit and advantage.

I have come a long way, and I believe I have been able to help a lot of people along the way. I am free to be me, and I am free from the need to control others.

Be Transformed, Not Conformed

Do not be conformed to this world (this age), [fashioned after and adapted to its external, superficial customs], but be transformed (changed) by the [entire] renewal of your mind [by its new ideals and its new attitude], so that you may prove [for yourselves] what is the good and acceptable and perfect will of God, even the thing which is good and acceptable and perfect [in His sight for you].

Romans 12:2

God's will for us is transformation, which takes place from the inside out. Conformation, on the other hand, is striving to live up to someone else's external, superficial idea of what we should be through our own effort to conform to their ideas, expectations and demands.

Often the world wants to draw the borders of a box for

us and put us in it. The problem is, the box is their design, not God's.

I can never be happy and fulfilled living in someone else's box, and neither can you.

Most people think we should do what they are doing—be part of their plan. This is wonderful if God agrees, but when God says no, we must learn to say no. We must also learn to say yes when He says yes.

People have skillfully developed methods of saying in a round-about way, "If you don't do what we want you to do, then we will reject you." Parents say it to their children, wives say it to husbands and husbands say it to wives. Congregations say it to their pastors. Friends say it to friends. It exists widely in every type of relationship.

The pain of rejection is hard to bear; therefore, we are very tempted to simply comply rather than to stand for our freedom. We can quickly become people-pleasers instead of God-pleasers (Eph. 6:6). Then we are not happy. There is no peace and no joy. We are not enjoying anything, and often we don't even know why.

We must be led by the Spirit if we are to enjoy the journey. We cannot be led, or controlled, by our friends, relatives or any other person in our lives.

Sometimes when we finally see that someone has been controlling us, we get very angry with that person about all the years of our lives he or she has stolen from us. God had to show me, when I was in the anger stage, that it was just as much my fault as the other person's.

Nobody can control us if we do not permit it. Sometimes we are so tense and fearful around others—so concerned that we won't impress them—that it makes us totally miserable. It also steals our confidence and keeps us from using the gifts that God has given us.

One night before one of our conferences, I went to the prayer room and found my worship leader doing stretching exercises. I thought to myself, "Now what's he doing? He's supposed to be getting ready to lead worship."

He saw me looking at him and said, "The Lord told me today when I was preparing for tonight to be loose." What he said struck me because I was teaching on liberty that night, and the first definition I had found in my study for the word "liberty" was to be loose!

When you get around other people, whether it is people you know or don't know, resist the temptation to be tense. Just relax, and loosen up. Be free to be yourself. If your friends will not allow you to be yourself, are they really your friends?

God was saying to Chris, our worship leader, "Don't feel pressured to perform."

The thief comes to kill (John 10:10). What does he desire to kill? The life of Christ that's in us. He wants to stifle and suffocate it with fear and insecurities.

I talked at length earlier in the book about legalism and

how if we live under the Law, it steals the life from us. The letter kills, but the Spirit gives life (2 Cor. 3:6). If we are not careful, we can allow other people to become a law to us.

Live and Let Live

"Live and let live" is a phrase that was designed to say, "Let's all be free." It means, "You mind your business, and I'll mind mine—and vice versa."

Did you know that even the Bible tells us that we should mind our own business?

> ...Make it your ambition and definitely endeavor to live quietly and peacefully, to *mind your own affairs,* and to work with your hands....
> 1 Thessalonians 4:11 (emphasis added)

This is something we all should strive to do. It should be our ambition to mind our own business.

I have definitely discovered that the application of this principle helps me greatly in enjoying my life.

Many times we get into things that were really none of our business to begin with, and those very things make us miserable. The Holy Spirit will not equip us to handle someone else's affairs. That is why things get so messy when we get involved where we should not be. There is obviously a place to get involved and help someone in need, but we need to be led by the Holy Spirit as to what we do and how we do it.

I have come to the place where I feel that I have enough business of my own to mind without getting involved in other people's.

It is amazing how our joy and enjoyment can increase just by following this one simple principle. I am very much in favor of the gifts of the Spirit, and a word of wisdom or knowledge (2 Cor. 12:8) can really encourage and help us press forward.

Just be sure if you have a "word" for someone that it is a word from God and not a word from you. Even the precious gifts of the Holy Spirit have been abused, and people have used them to manipulate and control others.

When someone gives you a word from God, always remember that it should be a confirmation of what the Lord has already shown you. If it is news to you, put it "on the shelf" in your thoughts and wait to see what God shows you about it.

Train Up a Child

Train up a child in the way he should go [and in keeping with his individual gift or bent], and when he is old he will not depart from it.

Proverbs 22:6

We must train our children. It is our responsibility before God to do so. Knowing their different personalities helps a great deal in doing it properly. When we compare the younger to the older, saying things like, "Why can't you get good grades like your sister?" and a variety of other things, we may be messing in God's business. He created each of our children and put them together for His purpose, not for ours.

Many parents want to fulfill their own unfulfilled dreams through their children, which creates a lot of pressure. Children naturally want to please their parents, but controlling parents will end up with rebellious children.

We must teach our young children what is right, but as they get older, we must also allow them to make their own choices. This will help develop a relationship of respect. They will not only respect us as their parents, but they will also respect our values, and ultimately, will be more willing to follow those values.

We as human beings are simply not built for outside control, and when it is forced on us, it creates problems.

When my daughters were growing up, I had certain ideas, certain standards, of what I thought a clean house should be. I tried to teach my girls to be clean and neat.

One of them had a personality that did not seem to mind messes, while the other one was even more neat than I was. I fought with the one and thought the other went a little overboard. Both are grown and now have homes of their own.

All three of us have varying definitions for the word "clean." One of my daughters is a little looser in her attitude. She enjoys her home—and it is clean—but she doesn't mind things lying around. She's the one who lives in it, so she is free to keep it as she sees fit.

The other daughter is fairly strict about how she wants things to look, but she is the one who cleans it, so that is her business.

I am probably somewhere between the two. I like my house to be a little more organized than my one daughter's, but it does not have to be as organized as the other's.

I realize now that I lost a lot of enjoyment when the girls were growing up because I was trying to make them be like me.

In order to give people freedom, we must realize they will never be good at being anyone other than themselves.

I struggled mightily with my older son when he was growing up, and I never knew until a few years ago that we struggled because we have identical personalities—both very strong. I felt that he was always resisting everything I said or did. I thought he was just rebellious, and his attitude did grow into a form of rebellion.

However, had I known how to give him some freedom (and I might add that strong-willed children need even more freedom than other types), we could have avoided a lot of turmoil between us. My strong personality and his were working against each other, but now through Christ (and both of us learning balance), we work together all the time in the ministry.

God once told me, "Lighten up on your kids, Joyce."

I want to encourage you not to be overly rigid with your children. They have not had time to learn what you know. Give them some time, and you will be surprised what God will teach them.

We cannot make our children love God, or make them want to do right. Naturally we must correct them, but we should avoid controlling them. We should bring correction when we are led by the Spirit—not by our flesh.

I have found with our children, our employees or anyone else under my authority, if I correct when I really need to, and not just when I want to, the results are much better.

Make a decision today that you are going to enjoy yourself and all the people that God has placed in your life. Don't just look at what is wrong with you, or with them. Be positive, look for the good things and magnify them.

Pray and ask God to help you live in the freedom you can have in Christ, and give the people in your life liberty to be who He has created them to be. As you do, you'll enjoy your relationships more than ever before!

13

Don't Poison Your Joy

For let him who wants to enjoy life and see good days [good—whether apparent or not] keep his tongue free from evil and his lips from guile (treachery, deceit).

1 Peter 3:10

The born-again child of God has joy living in his or her spirit. It is possible, however, to poison that joy.

The Scripture quoted above says that if we want to enjoy our lives, which is possible even if there is no apparent reason to enjoy them, then we must keep our tongues free from evil.

I believe the Scripture is a personal one: *You* keep *your* tongue free from evil.

When *The Amplified Bible* says that we can **enjoy life and see good days [good—whether apparent or not]**, I think it means that if we keep our words and thoughts positive during difficulties, though it may look to everyone else that our circumstance should make us miserable, we can drink joy from the fountain of our own lips.

The Fountain of Blessings and Curses

But the human tongue can be tamed by no man. It is a restless (undisciplined, irreconcilable) evil, full of deadly poison.

With it we bless the Lord and Father, and with it we curse men who were made in God's likeness!

Out of the same mouth come forth blessing and cursing. These things, my brethren, ought not to be so.

Does a fountain send forth [simultaneously] from the same opening fresh water and bitter?

James 3:8-11

We can bless ourselves or curse ourselves by the way we speak. When we bless, we speak well of; when we curse, we speak evil of. You and I can bless our own lives and bring joy to them, or we can curse them and bring misery upon ourselves, by the words of our mouth.

We should be much more concerned about what comes out of our mouths about ourselves than we ever are about what others are saying about us. There is a well of good things inside of us—one of them being joy. We can pull it up and splash it all over ourselves through proper speaking.

The Bible says the human tongue can be tamed by no man, so we will need God's help, and plenty of it, to keep the tongue under control.

In James 3:6 we read that **the tongue is a fire. [The tongue is a] world of wickedness set among our members, contaminating and depraving the whole body....**

It is amazing to stop and realize all the trouble that one tiny member of the body has created in each of our lives. The tongue can ruin a relationship. It can usher in depression. It can wound a friend, or, through rudeness, hurt someone we barely know.

Verse 8 in James 3 goes on to say that the tongue is...a **restless, (undisciplined, irreconcilable) evil, full of deadly poison.** Hmmmmm. Has your joy been poisoned?

If so, consider these Scriptures:

The words of a whisperer or slanderer are like dainty morsels or words of sport [to some, but to others are like deadly wounds]; and they go down into the innermost parts of the body [or of the victim's nature].

Proverbs 26:22

Death and life are in the power of the tongue, and they who indulge in it shall eat the fruit of it [for death or life].

Proverbs 18:21

Both of these Scriptures partially express the message I am trying to convey in this chapter: Words can help us or hurt us, as well as the other people we are involved with.

Agree with God, Not with the Trials

Do two walk together except they make an appointment and have agreed?

Amos 3:3

God has a good plan for our lives, and we need to bring our words and thoughts into agreement with Him. If we go around saying things like, "Nothing good ever happens to me; all I ever have is trouble," we can expect that trouble will multiply in our lives.

Words are seeds. What we speak, we sow, and what we sow, we reap! (See Gal. 6:7.)

Begin to say, "I've got a future, and there's hope for me. God is on my side. No matter how many disappointments I have had in the past, this is a new day. Goodness and mercy are following me today."

Talking like this will help you enjoy the journey. However long you have to wait for your breakthrough, you may as well make it as enjoyable as possible.

Keep yourself happy by being careful about what comes out of your mouth. Have you complained today? That will decrease your joy quickly.

Some people are "chronically critical." Have you said negative and judgmental things about someone else? That will certainly poison your joy. Unkind comments about other people cause us much more trouble than we know.

I was having some trouble one time with the anointing on my life. I felt something was hindering or blocking me. It was hard to explain, but something just was not right. This feeling persisted for about three weeks, and I finally knew I needed an answer from God.

He showed me that I had made a critical comment about another minister's preaching. I had said that it did not have any continuity to it—that he jumped all over the place. I had offended the Holy Spirit. This brother was a servant of God, preaching through the leading of the Holy Spirit, and I was judging his style.

We judge what is different, and usually because it challenges us. If this man's style was correct, maybe mine was the one that needed improvement. I did not consciously think that, but I do believe that often the insecurities we have about ourselves are the root of judgments brought against others.

I learned an important lesson from that incident. God really dealt very severely with me concerning this issue, and I know that part of the reason is because I am a teacher of His Word. He does not want bitter water coming out of the fountain one time, and sweet water the next time. He does not want me to praise Him and curse those made in His image.

Proverbs 18:21 says, **Death and life are in the power of the tongue, and they who indulge in it shall eat the fruit of it [for death or life].** Remember to keep your words sweet so that their fruit is sweet!

Conclusion
Finish Your Course with Joy

But none of these things move me; neither do I esteem my life dear to myself, if only I may finish my course with joy....

Acts 20:24

The Bible is full of Scriptures about joy, rejoicing, gladness and singing. One of my favorites is Psalm 100:1-2:

Make a *joyful* noise to the Lord, all you lands! Serve the Lord with *gladness!* Come before His presence with *singing!* (emphasis added)

Serving the Lord with gladness is a good goal for all of us. Often, we think we must do something great to please God, and we forget the simple things that obviously bless the Lord. It means a great deal to Him that His children serve Him with gladness.

There were many years when I had a ministry, but not much joy. I have since learned that the Lord would rather I have a glad heart than be successful, unless I can be both.

In years past at my conferences, I would ask people who were in full-time ministry but who were not enjoying their ministry to come to the altar for prayer. I was astonished at how many came forward each time that altar call was made.

It made me wonder: So many people are headed somewhere, but how many are enjoying the trip? It would be a great tragedy indeed to arrive and realize that the journey had not been enjoyed completely.

I agree with the apostle Paul: I want to finish my course *with joy.* This particular verse seems to speak deeply to my soul. What an awesome goal: to serve the Lord with gladness, and to complete our course with joy.

Since I am the determined type, I have always been determined to complete my course. But in the past few years I have added something extra to my original goal. Now, I not only want to complete my course, but I want to complete it *with joy.*

I pray that you feel the same way. Whatever your present situation is in life, whatever God has put in your heart to do, wherever you are called to go, enjoy the journey. Enjoy every single day. Don't waste one day of the precious life God has given you.

Rejoice in the Lord always [delight, gladden yourselves in Him]; again I say, *Rejoice!* Philippians 4:4

BIBLIOGRAPHY

Exley, Richard. *Rhythm of Life.* Tulsa: Honor Books, 1987.

Strong, Dr. James. *The New Strong's Exhaustive Concordance of the Bible.* Nashville: Thomas Nelson Publishers, 1990.

Vine, W. E., Unger, Merrill F., and White, William Jr. *Vine's Complete Expository Dictionary of Old and New Testament Words.* Nashville: Thomas Nelson, Inc., Publishers, 1985.

Webster's Ninth New Collegiate Dictionary. Springfield, MA: Merriam-Webster, Inc., 1990.

Webster's II New College Dictionary. Boston: Houghton Mifflin Company, 1995.

Webster's II New Riverside University Dictionary. Boston: Houghton Mifflin Company, 1984, 1988, 1994.

NOTES

Chapter 2

1. James Strong, *The New Strong's Exhaustive Concordance of the Bible* (Nashville: Thomas Nelson Publishers, 1990), "Hebrew and Chaldee Dictionary," p. 38, entry #2416.
2. W.E. Vine, Merrill F. Unger, and William White Jr., *Vine's Complete Expository Dictionary of Old and New Testament Words* (Nashville: Thomas Nelson, Inc., Publishers, 1985), p. 367.

Chapter 3

1. James Strong, *The New Strong's Exhaustive Concordance of the Bible* (Nashville: Thomas Nelson Publishers, 1990), "Greek Dictionary of the New Testament," p. 21, entry #1161.

Chapter 4

1. *Webster's II New College Dictionary,* s.v. "joy." [4]Vine, p. 201.

Chapter 5

1. *Webster's II New Riverside University Dictionary,* s.v. "complicate."
2. *Webster's II New Riverside University Dictionary,* s.v. "complicated."
3. *Webster's II New Riverside University Dictionary,* s.v. "simple."
4. *Webster's Ninth New Collegiate Dictionary,* s.v. "conversation."
5. If you have not read my book titled, *If Not for the Grace of God,* I recommend that you do so. See the book list in the back of this book.

Chapter 6

1. (Tulsa: Honor Books, 1987), p. 36.
2. James Strong, *The New Strong's Exhaustive Concordance of the Bible* (Nashville: Thomas Nelson Publishers, 1990), "Greek Dictionary of the New Testament," p. 71, entry #5040.

Chapter 7

1. *Webster's II New Riverside University Dictionary,* s.v. "religion."
2. *Webster's II New Riverside University Dictionary,* s.v. "relationship."

Chapter 8

1. *Webster's II New Riverside University Dictionary,* s.v. "celebrate."

Do you have a real relationship with Jesus?

God loves you! He created you to be a special, unique, one-of-a-kind individual, and He has a specific purpose and plan for your life. And through a personal relationship with your Creator—God—you can discover a way of life that will truly satisfy your soul.

No matter who you are, what you've done, or where you are in your life right now, God's love and grace are greater than your sin—your mistakes. Jesus willingly gave His life so you can receive forgiveness from God and have new life in Him. He's just waiting for you to invite Him to be your Savior and Lord.

If you are ready to commit your life to Jesus and follow Him, all you have to do is ask Him to forgive your sins and give you a fresh start in the life you are meant to live. Begin by praying this prayer...

> *Lord Jesus, thank You for giving Your life for me and forgiving me of my sins so I can have a personal relationship with You. I am sincerely sorry for the mistakes I've made, and I know I need You to help me live right.*
>
> *Your Word says in Romans 10:9, "If you declare with your mouth, 'Jesus is Lord,' and believe in your heart that God raised him from the dead, you will be saved" (NIV). I believe You are the Son of God and confess You as my Savior and Lord. Take me just as I am, and work in my heart, making me the person You want me to be. I want to live for You, Jesus, and I am so grateful that You are giving me a fresh start in my new life with You today.*
>
> *I love You, Jesus!*

It's so amazing to know that God loves us so much! He wants to have a deep, intimate relationship with us that grows every day as we spend time with Him in prayer and Bible study. And we want to encourage you in your new life in Christ.

Please visit joycemeyer.org/salvation to request Joyce's book *A New Way of Living*, which is our gift to you. We also have other free resources online to help you make progress in pursuing everything God has for you.

Congratulations on your fresh start in your life in Christ! We hope to hear from you soon.

ABOUT THE AUTHOR

JOYCE MEYER is one of the world's leading practical Bible teachers. Her daily broadcast, *Enjoying Everyday Life*, airs on hundreds of television networks and radio stations worldwide.

Joyce has written more than a hundred inspirational books. Her bestsellers include *Power Thoughts*, *The Confident Woman*, *Look Great, Feel Great*, *Starting Your Day Right*, *Ending Your Day Right*, *Approval Addiction*, *How to Hear from God*, *Beauty for Ashes*, and *Battlefield of the Mind*.

Joyce travels extensively, holding conferences throughout the year and speaking to thousands around the world.

JOYCE MEYER MINISTRIES ADDRESSES

Joyce Meyer Ministries
P.O. Box 655
Fenton, MO 63026
USA
(636) 349-0303

Joyce Meyer Ministries—Canada
P.O. Box 7700
Vancouver, BC V6B 4E2
Canada
(800) 868-1002

Joyce Meyer Ministries—Australia
Locked Bag 77
Mansfield Delivery Centre
Queensland 4122
Australia
(07) 3349 1200

Joyce Meyer Ministries—England
P.O. Box 1549
Windsor SL4 1GT
United Kingdom
01753 831102

Joyce Meyer Ministries—South Africa
P.O. Box 5
Cape Town 8000
South Africa
(27) 21-701-1056

OTHER BOOKS BY JOYCE MEYER

The Power of Forgiveness
The Power of Simple Prayer
Power Thoughts
Power Thoughts Devotional
Reduce Me to Love
The Secret Power of Speaking God's Word
The Secrets of Spiritual Power
The Secret to True Happiness
Seven Things That Steal Your Joy
Start Your New Life Today
Starting Your Day Right
Straight Talk
Teenagers Are People Too!
Trusting God Day by Day
The Word, the Name, the Blood
Woman to Woman
You Can Begin Again

JOYCE MEYER SPANISH TITLES

Belleza en Lugar de Cenizas (Beauty for Ashes)
Buena Salud, Buena Vida (Good Health, Good Life)
Cambia Tus Palabras, Cambia Tu Vida (Change Your Words, Change Your Life)
El Campo de Batalla de la Mente (Battlefield of the Mind)
Como Formar Buenos Habitos y Romper Malos Habitos (Making Good Habits, Breaking Bad Habits)
La Conexión de la Mente (The Mind Connection)
Dios No Está Enojado Contigo (God Is Not Mad at You)